AT 8:30

SUSAN ... GOD

Date Loaned

JAN 1 4 1952

LADY IN THE DARK

she wa

Jenny made her mind up when

All's Well, Mademoiselle

ENSA

WHEN A GLAMOROUS and superlative star lets down her lustrous hair and writes about her romances, her marriages, her personal friends on and off the stage and winds it up with excerpts from her exciting war diary, it is bound to make good reading. Gertrude Lawrence takes us backstage from the time she danced to the barrel organ on London's drab sidewalks to the time she played a farewell to Canadian troops in Antwerp last September, singing amid the din of Von Rundstedt's mortars.

It all began one bank holiday in Brighton when little "Gertie" put a penny in the fortune-telling machine. Out came a slip of blue paper reading simply: "A star danced . . . and under it you were born." At ten she left school and began to make her own living. From pantomime to musical comedy, Gertrude Lawrence danced, laughed, and sang her way. There were tough times—shows sometimes failed, managers decamped with the actors' pay, and once Miss Lawrence became a barmaid to pay a board bill.

Thus begins a gallant, heart-warming story, the story of a woman who went from poverty and despair to become the toast of two continents. L. S. B. Shapiro, the seasoned war correspondent of the Canadian forces overseas, has written of Miss Lawrence: "Her work is characterized by ardor made effortless and by painstaking skill bathed in a soft light of spontaneity."

Working with E.N.S.A., the British U.S.O., Miss Lawrence covered the Western front. But she covered all fronts from the Riviera to St. James's Palace, from Mayfair to Broadway. Through stormy romances and bankruptcy she has risen to the peak of stardom. In A STAR DANCED, she tells her own remarkable story—a story spiked with anecdote and filled with warmth.

A STAR DANCED

Gertrude Lawrence

A STAR DANCED

DOUBLEDAY, DORAN AND CO., INC., GARDEN CITY, N. Y. 1945

PHOTOGRAPHS USED ON END PAPERS BY COURTESY OF PHILIPPE HALSMAN AND
LIFE MAGAZINE, NEW YORK; LUCAS & MONROE, INC., NEW YORK; VANDAMM
STUDIO, NEW YORK; BOB GOLBY, NEW YORK; CECIL BEATON, LONDON; SASHA,
LONDON; MABEL ROBEY, LONDON.

For Richard

A STAR DANCED

1

"LUNCH IN LONDON, the day after tomorrow. . . ."

The skipper dropped the words out of one corner of his
mouth without disturbing the cigarette in the other corner.
He disposed of some three thousand miles of atmosphere as
nonchalantly as you would toss a peanut shell over your
shoulder.

I blinked. But only once. After all, the past two days had
been so fantastic that this ultimate scene and conversation
on the brilliantly lighted airfield outside a city in one of the
Southern states, beside the big airliner which was to take me
to England in a scheduled thirty-six hours, seemed part and
parcel of the events that had been happening thick and fast
ever since the telephone woke me at seven o'clock one
morning.

The telephone had summoned me from a dream in which
Richard and I were running, hand in hand, down our own
narrow strip of Cape Cod beach into the ocean. Sleepily,
unwilling to let go of that dream, I reached for the receiver
and held it to my ear. New York calling. At Dennis, Cape
Cod, at seven o'clock of a May morning, New York seems
as far away as London or Timbuktu.

"Are you up?" the voice of my lawyer demanded crisply.
Knowing me as she does, this was purely a rhetorical

question which, I felt, did not require an answer. She went on: "Get up! Right away! Get yourself onto the first plane, or the first train, into New York. I've just had word from the Air Ministry in Washington that there is space for you on the British Airways plane leaving at midnight tomorrow. You're on your way."

After weeks of more or less patient waiting, repeated timid, pleading, urgent, and finally importunate requests to the authorities who rule such matters in Washington and London, and a rapid-fire barrage of telegrams, cables, and telephone calls, it had happened. At last I had permission to do what I had been wanting desperately to do for four years —go to England and do my bit on a tour for E.N.S.A. Though no one knew just when, everyone was aware that the invasion of Europe was imminent. More than anything in the world I wanted the opportunity to entertain the British and American troops who would soon be fighting in France.

Basil Dean, founder and director of E.N.S.A.—the British equivalent of the U.S.O.—had cabled, asking me to come; but getting a priority to make the crossing and getting a place aboard a plane had taken a lot of wire-pulling at the American end. Now, I was really on my way home to London which I had not seen in six years. I would see my old friends, or at least those who remained of that gay company after the Battle of Britain—those who weren't fighting in Italy or the Near and Far East, or on any one of the seven seas.

And I might see Richard.

That thought brought me out of bed and under the shower in one swift leap. From then on the next two days were one mad rush, winding up with the final leap to the airport.

And now here I was, ready to board the big airliner for the hop to Newfoundland. I caught my breath, and did my best to imitate the casual-almost-to-the-point-of-boredom air shown by all members of all the air forces I have ever met when they are about to take off on a mission.

I was assured of passage to Newfoundland, where we were due to land at 9:00 A.M. the next day. Whether there would be a place for me in the plane going on from there to Ireland remained disturbingly uncertain. We all joked about it, standing there beside the plane. The others were sure of their passage all the way to England. They were officials or had diplomatic passports and were bursting with priorities. But I had only a number-three priority, which guaranteed me nothing much more than leave to hitch-hike.

Ernest Hemingway was among the favored ones. I met him then for the first time. There is something about Mr. Hemingway that makes one think of a small boy—a rather mischievous small boy whose pockets are full of bits of string, old rusty nails, chewing gum, and maybe a pet toad or two. A small boy hiding behind a big, bushy beard. He asked me, grinning:

"Suppose there is no place for you on the plane? What will you do?"

"Stow away," I retorted, "in your beard!"

This, I found, was Hemingway's first visit to England. How strange and sad, too, I thought, to have one's first glimpse of London in her grim battle dress.

My first view of Newfoundland, from about five thousand feet, was of an enormous black-and-brown land splashed with snow, like a huge chocolate cake with white icing. All around was a calm, oily, gray sea and, overhead, a beautiful clear, cloudless sky. We had breakfast in the cabin of the plane before we docked. Then we went out to breathe the fresh, salty, fishy-smelling air, stretch our legs, and see the sights. The airport was full of Canadian, British, and American airmen from the planes which ferry steadily back and forth across the North Atlantic. You felt you were getting close to the fighting front, even though several thousand miles of ocean still stretched between Newfoundland and Europe. Here, everyone was engaged, in one way or another, in getting on with the war. The little town was crowded. People spoke matter-of-factly about hopping from continent to continent.

Recalling letters from England and tales of food shortages over there, I did some prudent shopping and emerged triumphantly with a watch, which I had forgotten to get in New York, two pounds of butter, and a dozen eggs. I tried to buy some lemons, which I knew were regarded in England as extinct, but they were extinct that day in Newfoundland also.

The local paper announced that the Germans were retreating in Italy. Good! The invasion of Europe was believed to be very near now. And it was reported that Roosevelt would run again. I wished my chances of holding my seat (in the plane) were as good as his.

After lunch and the arrival of the Pan-American Clipper, bringing more passengers bound for England, I was assured there was a place for me on the plane leaving at one-fifteen. I told Ernest Hemingway:

"Your beard is now safe from British invasion."

For the next eighteen hours, during eight of which I slept soundly, we flew so high, sometimes at an altitude of eight thousand feet, that there was nothing to see but clouds. How strange was the knowledge that far below was the stretch of tossing gray ocean I had crossed so many times since my first trip to America in 1924, when I came over with the cast of _Charlot's Revue_. Strange to think that, far below us, the American and British navies were patrolling those same waters to protect the convoys of transports and freighters which were plying back and forth with men and war matériel.

Just after daylight we had our first glimpse of Ireland— lush green fields and the heather-colored mountains of Connemara with the morning mists curling from their crests like ostrich feathers. Disturbingly peaceful it seemed after the warlike atmosphere one felt in Newfoundland. Fat white sheep grazed placidly in the fields that bordered the road by which we motored from Limerick. Several times our car slowed down to clear the road for the herds of young beef cattle, bound (as I hoped) eventually for England. Every letter I had had from friends at home had spoken wistfully of the past days of plenty. Though none of the writers complained, you read between the lines the same longing you see in children's faces pressed against a sweetshop window.

We took off again late that afternoon and put down at Croydon about seven o'clock. The skipper, who had promised me lunch in London that day, was only five hours out on his calculation.

Flying across southern England, I wondered where Richard was and how soon I might see him. After all, I couldn't expect the American Navy to adjust its plans to allow one of its lieutenant commanders to be at Croydon to meet his wife. But, being a woman, I couldn't help wishing.

In the excitement of actually recognizing the big, familiar field just below us, I bounced in my seat—and promptly broke two of the precious eggs in my lap.

"My God, woman," said Hemingway, helping me clean up the mess, "what are you going to do *now?*"

"Fortunately, I'm the same shape front and back," I told him. I jerked my tweed skirt around so that the egg stain was behind me, buttoned my fur coat, and assured myself, as I tripped down the gangplank, that I was making as neat an entrance as any in my career.

It was eight o'clock, the dinner hour, when I drove up to the dear familiar Savoy. It was not yet dark, just the beloved twilight, yet London's streets were strangely quiet and free of traffic. There were great gaps in the familiar skyline and piles of rubble along the streets we drove through. All the way over I had been steeling myself for this, my first view of bombed London. I knew it was going to be hard to take. There was bound to be that wrenching struggle between the impulse to cry out and the feeling that one simply dared not give way to one's feelings. London is my home town. I was born there in Kennington Oval. I grew up within the sound of Bow Bells. I spoke with a cockney accent until I was eleven or thereabouts, when Miss Italia Conti scolded and drilled me out of it. In London I have been by turns poor and rich, hopeful and despondent, successful and down and out, utterly miserable and ecstatically, dizzily happy. I belong to London as each of us can belong to only one place on this earth. And, in the same way, London belongs to me.

The windows of my room at the Savoy looked out over the Thames Embankment. After a solitary dinner, as I stood there looking down, I had my first sharp realization of what war had done to my town. An impenetrable black curtain seemed to have fallen between me and the city. The enveloping blackness in which the stars seemed unreally bright and near and the unusual, wary, listening stillness were more impressive at that moment than the destruction wrought by the bombs. They filled me with a swift, blinding fury against the enemy who could muffle the voice and force of the greatest and most tolerant city in the world. Suddenly the silence overhead was cut by the whir of flying planes. They were our bombers starting out for targets across the Channel. The sound carried me back to World War I, when we used to be glad of nights such as this, when there was no moon to guide the Zeppelins up the winding Thames to drop their death freight on us.

On such a night . . .

Suddenly, as against a black-velvet backdrop, the past came back to me, and I saw myself as a little girl, dancing on a sidewalk in Clapham. . . .

Clapham is not the least desirable of London's many widely sprawled districts. Clapham is "genteel." Dwellers in other suburban districts of London speak enviously of their better-off cousins and in-laws who are privileged to live in Clapham, London S.W. For them—and they include thousands of tried-and-true Londoners—Clapham is something to aspire to.

Residents of Clapham speak of these less-favored boroughs with no more than the faintest tinge of superiority.

For if there is one thing which every true Claphamite knows and will swear to, it is that employment is full of uncertainties and life is a matter of ups and downs. His attitude toward the dwellers in the East End is that of the humble apostle; but for the grace of God, there go I.

Clapham has its own code, its own proper pride, and its own firmly rooted conventions. For one thing, it is very bad form, indeed, to ask questions. Of course you can't help being aware of certain facts about your neighbors: the hours they keep, who is in or out of work, whose husband spends more of his free time at the corner pub than he spends with his family, and what they buy at the butcher's and greengrocer's. Good form, however, demands a pretense that you know none of these things. If one of your neighbors suddenly disappears overnight, bag and baggage, you are properly surprised about it the next morning, even though you did hear the bailiff's voice in the hall and the stamping made by the men from the hire-purchase company as they carried out the furniture.

If you were brought up in Clapham, as I was, you don't have to be informed of these nice points of etiquette. You grow up knowing them. "Don't be nosy," Mother would say. And Dad would add: "It doesn't pay to see everything, my girl."

Mother hadn't always lived in Clapham, and Kennington Oval was a step down for her. Her father had been a master builder—a man of substance in his own line, whose fortune, however, had been lost in "gilt-edged" securities. Granny still lived in the same house to which she had moved as a young bride, where her children were born, and where, she stoutly affirmed, she intended, "God willing, my dear," to die. Mother had taken a step down when she allowed the unexplained romantic streak in her nature to make her deaf to the dictates of her class. Following that will-o'-the-wisp, she married for love with a blind disregard for economic security—married, of all things, a theatrical! And a foreigner at that. Even though he had come to England at the age of two, he was a Dane whose professional name was Arthur Lawrence. He sang in a deep, rich basso profundo, and with a dramatic fervor that went down very well with audiences at smoking concerts and in the smaller music halls. He rendered such favorites as "Old Black Joe" and "Asleep in the Deep." His "Drinking Song" was famous throughout Brixton and Shepherd's Bush. Alas!

Mother had been very carefully brought up. "All the time your father courted me we never once were out together after ten o'clock. I'm sure I don't know what your grandfather would have said if I had not been home and on my way to bed when the clock struck that hour."

So much decorum must have been a great strain on my father, accustomed as he was to the hours kept by the profession. Perhaps something in his Danish nature responded to this strict middle-class propriety. His family, the Klasens, were a solid, respectable lot—and he was the only one of them with a taste for anything so Bohemian as the stage.

Mother's family shook their heads over the future of such a marriage, and they were quite right about it. My father liked his glass, and an evening dedicated to bass solos gives a man a thirst. He was—as I was to learn—one of those whose personality was completely altered by alcohol. His gaiety, his charm, his blond good looks disappeared. He became ugly in disposition and demeanor. Mother left him soon after I was born. I grew up with no memories and no knowledge of him. But I adored Dad, my stepfather.

No wonder Granny shook her head over Mother, who just couldn't seem to learn about men. Mother chose her two husbands for their charm, not for their ability to provide. Father had always been able to sing for our supper, but Dad was always promising to provide handsomely. "Wait," he would say to us. "Just let me back a winner. . . ." When he did, we would celebrate with a slap-up feast—boiled salmon, or a bird, toasted cheese, and a side dish of prawns. And, occasionally, asparagus. The first time we had this delicacy, I remember, Mother cut off all the green tips and boiled the white stalks.

Gertrude Alexandra Dagmar Lawrence Klasen—little Gertie Lawrence to you—was quite satisfied with Kennington Oval. For one thing, the organ-grinder came there frequently and would pause and grind out a tune on each side of the Oval, which gave the residents a fair-sized concert. I never could resist him, nor could I learn to be a proper child and satisfy myself with opening the window a crack to let the music come into the room.

"Where is that child?" Mother would ask. One look from the window was enough. There I was, following the organ down the street, holding out my brief skirts and dancing to what I hoped was the admiration of the neighbors.

Nobody that I know of had taught me to dance. The steps just seemed to come to me the minute my ears caught the music. But Mother loved "musical evenings," and my first song, learned from a sheet of free music cut from a newspaper, went like this:

Oh, it ain't all honey, and it ain't all jam,
Walking round the 'ouses with a three-wheel pram,
All on me lonesome, not a bit to eat,
Walking about on me poor old feet.
My old man, if I could find 'im,
A lesson I would give.
Poor old me, I 'aven't got a key,
And I don't know where I live.
Boom! Boom!

Whenever we had company, on a Sunday night, I would be made to oblige with a song. "Gertie's such a funny one!" Dad would puff out his chest, proud of my accomplishment.

"Fancy! A child her age singing songs like that!"

"Whatever will she do next? She ought to go on the stage. She's got it in her."

That song brought me the first money I ever earned. The summer I was six Dad must have had a streak of unusual good luck with the horses because he took Mother and me to Bognor Regis for the bank holiday. It was boiling hot, I remember, and the sands were crowded. I had never been to the sea before; the bathers, the picnic parties on the sand, the strollers along the Front fascinated me. A concert party was entertaining, and Dad paid for us to go in. At the close of the regular bill the "funny man" came forward and invited anyone in the audience who cared to, to come up on the stage and entertain the crowd. A push from Mother and the command: "Go on now, Gertie, and sing your song," was all the urging I needed. "*It ain't all honey, and it ain't all jam,*" I caroled lightly, twirling on my toes with my skimpy pink frock held out as far as it would stretch.

The applause and the cheers were gratifying, even without the large golden sovereign with which the manager rewarded me after a little speech.

I know I must have told this story to Noel Coward. No doubt I boasted of it when we were both pupils at Miss Conti's dancing school. The incident may have given him the idea for one of the scenes in *Cavalcade*. Anyway, I like to think so. In fact, when I saw the play, there was something so familiar about that little girl doing her song and dance on the Brighton sands, the little girl who grew up to be an actress, that I felt a rush of tears and a choke in my throat. She made me remember, suddenly, so many things I thought I had forgotten.

One other thing makes that holiday at Bognor Regis stand out in my mind. We were living in lodgings, of course. Late one Sunday afternoon Mother told Dad to take me for a walk along the Front while she got our supper ready. Dad and I walked about for a bit, enjoying the crowds; then I noticed that his steps began to drag and he began to cast longing eyes at the saloon doors from which, now that they were open again, came the cool, sour smell of beer. Finally, he could stand it no longer.

"Sit down on that bench, Gertie," he said. "You can have a nice look at the sea and the people going by. Be a good girl, now, and don't move until I come back for you."

I watched him disappear in the direction of the nearest bar. I was not disconcerted. Obediently I sat on the bench, swinging my legs and enjoying my freedom. Even more than the sea and the crowd, I was interested in a stand where a sign announced bicycles for hire. That drew me as inevitably as the saloon had drawn Dad.

"How much does it cost to hire a bike?" I asked.

"Sixpence an hour, my dear," said the attendant.

I felt around in my coat pocket and produced the coin. The attendant looked at me a bit doubtfully, but the sixpence was real enough and there in the rack was a bike just my size. He took it out and lifted me up on the saddle.

"That will do you a fair treat," he said. "Now be sure you bring it back in an hour." He turned away to wait on another customer.

I wheeled the machine proudly across the Front and down a street into a crescent where the railings in front of the houses gave me something to hold onto. I had never been on a bicycle before, but I had no doubt of my ability to ride one. I leaned it against the railing, paying no attention to the sign which read, "Fresh Paint," mounted it, and, holding onto the railing with one hand, managed to pedal around the crescent. It was thrilling, like riding a circus horse around the ring, and there was always the possibility that the people were watching me from the windows of the houses. I fell off several times, skinned my knee, and got the front of my frock grubby while the side toward the railings became ornamented with stripes of green paint, but I kept at it, getting better with each lap. I had forgotten Dad and Mother, even the admonition of the attendant at the bicycle stand to be back within an hour.

It was getting dusk before Dad found me, a frantic, red-faced, frightened Dad, who had already spent some time running up and down the Front calling, "Gertie! Gertie!" and demanding of everyone, "Have you seen my little girl anywhere about?"

His relief at sight of me was immediately transformed into anger for the fright I had caused him. "Now, then, whatever have you been up to? You'd ought to be ashamed of yourself running off like that! Such a fright you've given me! Whatever would I have said to your mother? She won't half give you a piece of her mind when she sees what you've done to your frock! And it's your poor dad will get the worst of it."

He went on, muttering and scolding, all the way back to the bicycle stand where he paid the attendant for the over-time. And still clutching me by the hand, as though afraid I would vanish again, he hurried me back to our lodgings. We were nearly there when he stopped, removed his hat, and wiped his brow. Giving me a long look that immediately established a confidence between us, he remarked tentatively, "I don't know. How would it be if we were to take your mother a little gin and bitters to have with her supper?"

I nodded approval.

"Wait here, then. And none of your vanishing acts, my girl!"

He stepped jauntily into the convenient door of a refreshment bar. After a few minutes he emerged, wiping his mustache and looking very much more like himself. He patted one bulging pocket: "Your mother always did fancy a gin and bitters. Your mother's a wonderful woman, Gertie. Don't you ever forget it!"

No, I promised him. Somehow or other I felt that I now had two allies against Mother's anger when she discovered the state of my dress. Dad, I felt, would be on my side and could be counted on to bring up the reinforcements—namely the gin and bitters—at the psychological moment.

Dad's admiration for Mother was unbounded, and his devotion was as great as his admiration. Whenever they had a tiff, he would feel moved to tell me solemnly that it was all his fault. He appreciated Mother's fine qualities, and he would lecture me on the subject of showing the same appreciation.

"Mind you always do as your mother tells you to, my girl. Your mother's a wonderful woman. Just you try to be like her, and you won't go far wrong."

There was nothing sentimental about Mother, nor about her determination to bring me up according to her standards. She saw to it that I came straight home from school each day and that I did the household tasks that were assigned to me. One of these was blacking the fire grates. As Mother said, there was something about a well-blacked grate that gave a room an air. It may be that this helped her morale and compensated for some of the instability of her life with Dad. Each of us has some sort of pet fetish, something we cling to which gives us self-confidence and power to go on. A neat, well-blacked fireplace was Mother's. If she had blacked the grates herself, she would have missed the satisfaction of feeling that she was bringing up her daughter in the proper tradition. So I blacked the grates each day. And on Saturdays I did the brass and helped in general.

It was not sentimentality but a fierce pride for herself and for Dad that made Mother put me into ruffled frocks which were a bother to make and to wash and iron. And what a nuisance they were for me to keep clean! It seemed as though some mischievous fate led me into trouble as soon as I was sent out, freshly bathed and dressed, with strict orders to "walk around the pond and try to act like

a little lady." It wasn't that I deliberately tried to be diso-
bedient, but that life would not let me follow Mother's
command. It would hold out some other inducement to
me, something I could not refuse. Before I knew it I would
be engaged in sailing boats on the pond, getting wetter and
muddier every minute, or making friends with some stray
puppy whose playful paws had no regard for my starched
ruffles.

"Why can't you be like your cousin Ruby!" Mother
would scold.

My cousin was all that I was not—she was a plump, pretty,
neat child with curls hanging to her waist; my hair was lank
and as straight as a die. My cousin Ruby was always spot-
less and without a wrinkle. Her nails were clean. She was
the pride of the family, and she knew it. Her father, my
mother's brother, was in charge of the Royal Stables at
Buckingham Palace, which gave Ruby a prestige.

"Just look at your cousin," Mother would say. "She is
such a credit to her parents, it's a pleasure to watch her
come into a room. Here I spend *hours* on making you look
nice and it lasts until you're out of sight. I declare, Gertie,
you've got the very devil in you."

I think Mother always regretted losing the world in which
she had lived briefly with my father—the world of the
theater. In a slightly discolored mother-of-pearl card case
she treasured a number of visiting cards of actresses she had
known in those days. Sometimes, as a treat, she would let me
play with them. I would pull a card out of the case, read the
name aloud, and she would immediately launch into the
story of how she and the owner of the card met and where,
what her specialty was, and Mother's own opinion of how

good she was at it. This parlor game gave me my first inside information on the theatrical profession. One of the things I learned was that Friday was "professional night" at most of the theaters. On Friday night it was usual to admit members of the profession free. By the time I was eight or nine, I had learned the trick of writing neatly across the face of any one of the cards, "Please give my little girl two seats." If Mother was out that evening, I would take the card, call for one of my little girl friends, and together we would take the tram to Brixton or any near-by district where there was a theater. I would present myself and my card at the box office. The man would look through the wicket at me a little doubtfully, whereupon I would put on my most innocent and pleading look. Usually someone hanging about would say: "Oh, give the kids a couple of seats." We would skip in and find places in the gallery.

After the show we would take the tram home, hoping desperately to get there before our mothers found us out. Once, I remember, either the tram was delayed or Mother came home from Granny's earlier than usual. She found the other little girl's mother hammering at our door.

"Your Gertie came and took my Mabel!" she cried. "They're not back yet."

Mother did not put off whipping me to ask questions. After the punishment, she began to inquire into our evening. What shocked her most of all was our riding to and from Brixton on the tram.

"Did you speak to anyone?" she demanded.

"A gentleman spoke to me."

"How do you know he was a gentleman?" Mother asked suspiciously.

"Because he was wearing a gold watch and chain!"

Strangely, this seemed to satisfy her as completely as it had satisfied me.

The rooms on Kennington Oval marked the high tide of our finances. We lived there only as long as luck was with Dad. Then we moved, as we frequently did. There was a regular ritual connected with these movings which varied only as we moved up or down in the economic scale. If the move was occasioned by good fortune, Mother added a piano to the furniture she ordered sent around to the new address. There was something undeniably genteel about a piano in the house, even if no one could play it.

If the move was in the other direction, a van drove up and men smelling of sawdust and beer carried away the piano and the rest of the furniture which we had on the hire-purchase plan. They were quite impersonal about it; they gave us to understand that their orders to take away the tables and chairs and the sideboard with the mirror at the back came from the company. Mother was always on her dignity with them. She refused to be commiserated with. In her own way she contrived to imply a disdain for the household chattels over which there was such an unaccountable to-do. The impersonal air with which she watched the men from the Hire Furniture Company stagger down the front steps under the pseudo-Jacobean fumed-oak dresser was a triumph of dramatic genius. As the rooms became emptier, you felt that Mother was merely clearing her decks for bolder action, and that when we had furniture again, it would be on a nobler, more elegant scale.

Meanwhile Dad would have slipped 'round the corner and entered into negotiations with the neighborhood greengrocer whose account had been paid up and whose friend-ship could therefore be relied upon. Not until after dark, when there would be no prying eyes, would Mother take down the window curtains and pack the few possessions rightfully our own and which remained constant through all the changes for better or for worse—the bedding, though not the beds, the kitchen pots and pans, the square black marble-and-gilt clock with the figure of Britannia resting on her shield staring pensively at a beast which resembled a poodle more than a lion, the pair of gaily-flowered Royal Worcester vases which always flanked the clock above every hearth we gathered round, and a red glass mug en-graved with the date of Queen Victoria's Jubilee.

Close on to midnight the grocer's boy would arrive with his cart. Dad would tiptoe down the stairs with the parcels and baskets and pile them on the cart while the boy leaned against the railing and kept a lookout for "Nosy Parkers." In all this there was nothing original; we were merely fol-lowing a tradition long recognized in Clapham and in other less-favored districts. This maneuver was known in the vernacular as a "moonlight flit." Obviously, it was a move to cheaper lodgings in another district where we and our straitened circumstances were as yet unknown. Also, obvi-ously, it was without the landlord's knowledge.

There must have been families whose moonlight flits were sad and shamefaced. Not ours. There was something daring and whimsical about this sort of move which challenged all that was adventurous in our three natures. Each of us responded to the challenge differently; each in his own way.

Mother always dressed up to the nines for the occasion. She would skewer her largest birded hat atop her puffs, twine a marabou boa elegantly about her neck, and draw on a pair of long, worn, but carefully mended gloves. Catching up her skirt with one hand and carrying the tea-kettle in the other, she would sweep down the stairs with a dignity calculated to overpower any lurking landlord.

In Dad, jauntiness rose over dignity. He would cock his bowler at an angle, and thumbs in the armholes of his waistcoat, he would chaff the grocer's boy, making him a partner in the adventure.

At a signal from Dad the boy would push off with his cart, Dad would gallantly offer Mother his arm, and they would follow. I would bring up the rear of the little procession. So we moved through Clapham's silent streets, pioneers setting forth into the unknown to start a new home in a new and untried land. Adventure tingled in my toes. Where the moon or a street lamp splashed the pavement with light, my feet would begin to dance. . . .

2

THE SUN WAS SHINING when I opened my eyes on my first morning glimpse of London. Immediately things began to happen. Phones rang, flowers arrived, photographers snapped cameras at me, and the press began asking how it felt to be home again after six years "in the States."

I could tell them in one word: wonderful.

All that day and through the week that followed, lunching, teaing, and dining with old friends, applying to the proper bureaus for ration cards, gas mask, tin hat (quite fetching when worn at just the right tilt), and a National Service Permit to enter restricted areas, I was discovering and making acquaintance with a London that was strange to me.

I thought I knew London in every possible mood—gay and handsome and smart and ceremonious as she was during the coronation summer of 1937. I was there for that brilliant high tide of midsummer pomp. Officially I was "resting" while Rachel Crothers rewrote and polished *Susan and God*. Actually, I was entertaining myself and being entertained by the gayest season London had had in many years and the last she was to see for a long time to come. During those weeks, when the old city was washed and brushed and bedecked, like a doting grandmother for the marriage of a favorite grandson, all of us drank deep of our pleasure. Perhaps we had a premonition of what lay just ahead. Anyway, that London of 1937 came the closest to Edwardian London of any other season since World War I.

The year before I had been playing in *Tonight at 8:30*. All that season there was a hush over England; people spoke softly, nobody made plans. Everyone waited for the bulletins which gave us news of the King's condition. We felt the imminent passing of an era. I had a small radio in my dressing room at the theater and would turn it on between acts to pick up the news from the B.B.C. The news, to everyone in England that year, meant one thing—news of the King.

One night when we knew the King was very low, Douglas Fairbanks, Jr., was in my dressing room waiting for the final curtain. When I came off the stage and into the dressing room, the radio was tuned in and I didn't need to ask questions. Douglas' face told me that the last bulletin had not held out much hope. Very quickly I changed, and Douglas and I took a taxi to Buckingham Palace. It was impossible to get close, because the Mall and all the wide space in front of the gates were so crowded. Thousands of Londoners and people up from the country were packed shoulder to shoulder in a silent, motionless mass. We joined the others and waited.

I remember seeing Claire Luce, in a bright scarlet coat, wedged into the crowd. She was then playing in *The Gay Divorce*, and she had come just as she stepped off the stage, even with her make-up on.

There was nothing one could do, but somehow there was no other place one wanted to be at that moment. Every quarter of an hour or so someone came out of the palace and posted a new bulletin on the board fastened to the gates. Then the whole crowd moved forward as one man. The two or three in a position to read the typewritten notice passed the word back. The message rippled through the crowd: "The King is sinking." I held on very tight to Douglas' arm and he to mine. We were rumored as being engaged, but just then and there personal relationships did not count for much.

Presently a new notice was put on the board. Again that urgent sweep forward of the crowd, like the tide pushing its way into a cove. But this time there was no ripple or whisper. Silently those in the front rank stepped back and removed their hats; then from the crowd as from one man there rose a single sigh.

We were wedged too close to turn. I was squeezed between Douglas and another very tall young man. I saw him sweep off his hat. There were tears running down his cheeks.

"Well, I guess that's that," he said. His voice told me he was an American.

The words wrote an end to a chapter.

The big event of my first day was getting in touch with Richard. He phoned he could get leave and asked me to come down and meet him at his base the next day, which was Saturday. We arranged that I would take the nine-thirty train from Waterloo. I arrived at the station a good half-hour beforehand only to be told the train had been canceled in the night. As no one seemed to think this was unusual, I got the impression that train schedules were pretty uncertain things even though the traffic was described as normal. I went back to the hotel and filled in time until I should start for the next train, which was scheduled to leave at eleven-thirty. However, I allowed myself plenty of time and took up my stand at gate No. 10 as the station guard had instructed me to do. There were so few people standing there I thought I was in luck, but this optimism was immediately shattered by a voice from the loud-speaker which announced: "Passengers waiting for the eleven-thirty to Portsmouth will please join the queues by the boards marked '5' and '6.' " Before these gates stretched two apparently endless queues, one made up of servicemen—British, American, Canadian; the other, of civilians. I added myself to the tail of the latter queue and waited with what patience I could muster. Slowly the procession shuffled a few steps nearer the still-distant gate. I kept my eye on my Newfoundland watch while my hopes of joining Richard that day evaporated. At eleven-thirty the voice spoke again: "The eleven-thirty is now full. The twelve forty-five has been canceled. The next train leaves at one-thirty."

I dropped out of line and set about planning a campaign. I dashed back to the near-by Savoy, where I changed into my American Red Cross uniform; then I returned to Waterloo Station and elbowed my way into the queue with the armed forces. After standing in line an hour and a half, I found a place on the one-thirty train.

It was quite an experience, but worth it. Richard met me. After many months of service overseas, he, apparently, was quite philosophic about trains which do not run and, when they do, cannot accommodate all of the passengers. We had a lovely day together and I returned to London the next morning. I was still wearing my Red Cross uniform and having lunch in the Savoy Grill when who should come along but Basil Dean. He stared at me.

"What are you doing in that uniform, Gertie?"

I explained. Whereupon he commanded me to go at once and be fitted for an E.N.S.A. uniform. Having known Basil since I was a child when he "managed" me, I meekly obeyed.

At first there seemed to be a great deal of hush-hush about the unit to which I was to be assigned, where we were to go, and—most important of all—when we were to start. All I could find out was that we were headed for an eight-weeks tour of Great Britain, during which we would be called on to give three shows a day, with a lot of motoring between shows.

Rehearsals were called in one of the underground cellars of Drury Lane Theatre, which had been bombed during the blitz, but which was still the E.N.S.A. headquarters.

At the first rehearsal I learned that ours was to be known as The Gertrude Lawrence Unit, a tremendous honor and one which made me feel a bit shy and self-conscious, especially as the others in the unit had all been together since the opening of E.N.S.A. But the ice was quickly broken over a couple of beers, and soon everyone was talking shop as pros do when and wherever they get together.

The only non-professional among us was Mary Barrett, whose position in the unit was that of shepherd, manager, confidential adviser, trouble-shooter, and bodyguard. Surely, that should give her professional rating. Mary had been Gracie Fields' secretary-companion when Gracie was in England, and consequently she knew the ropes. She could improvise a costume at the last minute if the wardrobe trunks failed to turn up. With equal skill and speed, she could contrive to cook a supper over a gas ring out of whatever the shops or the rations offered. She had the soothing tact of a career diplomat and the adroitness of a ward politician. No one ever heard her grouse or complain of weariness, lack of sleep, or even the temperament of us performers.

We put on our first show and a big B.B.C. broadcast at a factory in Ilford on the outskirts of London for twenty-five hundred workers. The plant turned out radio parts for planes and was working at full production speed. The show gave me a chance to try out some of the songs I had brought over from America, but while I realized that these factory workers were doing a tremendously important job, nevertheless it was the troops I had come over to sing to. I was impatient to start our tour of the camps.

Meanwhile, during the week of waiting, I was discovering more things about the British people than I had ever thought about before.

I heard very little talk about the war. In fact, I rather got the idea no one was expected to talk about it. Perhaps this was because everyone—men and women—was doing some sort of war service. Everybody had to do fire watching on the roofs. Nobody whined about the servant problem, because there weren't any servants to whine about. A maid might be allowed to a household in which a certain number of persons were billeted. Otherwise people were doing their own housework, cooking their own meals, and making a practice of eating out whenever possible.

Shopping took endless time. I saw Londoners of every social class queueing up for hours in front of the fish shops. The streets were full of bicycles. Everyone cycled to and from his job. The boots that pressed the pedals were patched on the soles, but they were well polished. This meant that the wearer had done the polishing himself. That below-stairs character so dear to Dickens and to the writers and illustrators of *Punch*—I mean the British "boots"—had joined up, or was making munitions.

People looked very fit, especially the women, most of whom were in some sort of uniform—the WRENS, ATS, Red Cross, et cetera. Everyone was busy all the time, but there was no rush or excitement. No one was breathless. You felt that without deliberate effort or any bravado everyone was carrying on the accustomed pattern of life as consistently as possible.

London was full of American correspondents. They kept popping up wherever you went. Allan Michie, who was commissioned to cover the invasion for the *Reader's Digest*, Liebling of the *New Yorker*, Hemingway on an assignment for *Collier's*, and several others I ran into, were fuming because word had gone around that they would not be allowed to go across with the British forces. General Eisenhower had apparently given permission, but some liaison officer on the staff said there was no room for them, so they were muttering and squabbling. I was a sympathetic listener. I heard many accounts of the early days of the Battle of Britain. For instance, there was the story that during the early days of home-guard training the men were given beer bottles—three apiece—filled with some kind of mild explosive. With these homemade grenades they were expected to knock out the German tanks as they advanced up the beaches. These were the famous "Molotov Cocktails."

Things were different now. Munitions in more formidable quantities were being turned out by the war plants for the invasion of Europe. Ernest Byfield, acting as war correspondent for the Hearst press, told me it took ten thousand pairs of nylon stockings to make one towrope for a glider plane, and at least a thousand gliders are needed for an air-borne invasion. "That should be broadcast to the black-market shoppers in America and elsewhere."

I agreed.

"When peace comes, instead of beating swords into plowshares, I suppose we will convert our towropes into stockings."

"And our tin hats into ash trays," I added.

We laughed about it, but, actually, we had learned the British way of thinking, which is that, no matter how the war is going, and in spite of the changes it imposes on everybody, the day will inevitably come when the established, comfortable, peaceful life, which every British person considers no more than his due, will return.

I was made aware of this national psychology the evening I went to dine with Daisy Neame in Eaton Square. On my way there I passed a sign which read: "Horse Shelter." That is something I am sure could exist only in Great Britain. I spoke of it at dinner and was told that the regulations regarding the treatment of animals during air raids were very strict. When the alert sounds, horses must be unharnessed immediately from carts and led to designated places of shelter before the driver takes cover.

Somehow one felt behind those horse shelters the sport-
ing instincts of the British, as well as the indomitable hu-
manitarianism of all those tenderhearted ladies who used
to write letters to the *Times* regarding the treatment of
animals. It would take a lot more than the German blitz to
lessen the British sense of responsibility toward horses,
dogs, cats, birds, donkeys, and all domestic animals.

The war has altered some aspects of British life unbeliev-
ably. Daisy's door was opened by her husband Lionel. But-
lers have become extinct, even in Eaton Square. Everything
was as I remembered it except for three unusual vehicles
standing in the hall. These were the two bicycles on which
Lionel and Daisy pedal to their respective war jobs. The
third was the baby's pram which Daisy told me she wheeled
herself, to give the infant an airing, when she went out to
do the marketing. Another innovation in Mayfair. The British "nannies" in their correct gray uniforms and caps with
flaring streamers have disappeared out of London's life for
the duration.

When we went in to dinner the table looked just as lovely
as usual. The silver had the wonderful blue sheen that
comes only from frequent vigorous polishings. The damask
was lustrous, and the centerpiece of heavy-headed tulips
was like a cluster of glowing jewels. The men, of course,
were in uniform. Daisy and I wore short black dresses. Yes,
it was all almost prewar. But one thing was missing—there
were no servants to wait on us.

We finished the first course. "Here we go," said Daisy,
rising and leading the way to the sideboard. She slid back
the shutter of a little window she had had cut in the wall

between the dining room and the service pantry. Daisy went around into the pantry and received the plates each of us passed to her through the window; then she handed us plates with the next course, which we carried back to the table and proceeded to eat with enjoyment. Daisy had cooked the meal herself, and I must say she had done a very good job.

I found a tremendous interest in America—a genuine curiosity about what Americans thought, what they were doing, and how they felt about the British. Everything sent from the U.S.A. had become extraordinarily valuable and desirable. I don't suppose that at any time since the reign of James I, when the first British colonies were established in America, has the world beyond the Atlantic held out such riches as it does today.

The British are rediscovering America. And vice versa.

Later, thinking over the things I had seen going about London, I began to ask myself why I took this imperturbability without surprise. Because I wasn't surprised by it at all. Somehow or other, deep down in me, was the knowledge that of course these people would act in exactly this way. What would have surprised me would have been to find them forsaking their ideals of behavior and their standards of what is pleasant, enjoyable, and worth fighting for.

Inherently and instinctively I knew these things about the British people because I had known and loved Granny. Though her life was lived a very long stone's throw from Mayfair, Granny, nevertheless, was a perfect personification of the British character. She represented the backbone of the nation.

"Mark my words, Alice, the child has talent."

Whenever Granny said "mark my words," she became the family oracle, to be heard and heeded with respect.

She spoke composedly, continuing to rock in her wheel-back armchair with her feet resting on the brass fender rail, while her knitting needles clicked without ceasing.

I have no way of knowing just when Granny decided that I was destined for the theater. She and Grandfather, whom I chiefly remember because he suffered from a disease called chalky gout, had strongly disapproved of their daughter Alice's alliance with the profession. Perhaps they accepted the fact that the offspring of that unfortunate union was doomed from the moment of conception, and could not, therefore, be held back from her dark destiny. At any rate, I never remember Granny putting up any objections to my frankly expressed ambition to go on the stage.

To tell the truth, she encouraged me. Whenever I stayed with her we would play theater. The program started with me coming through the sitting-room door to bow to her as the audience and make my opening speech which began: "Ladies and gentlemen, I am about to appear." I would then disappear and get dressed up for the performance.

During those early years, when our family finances went up and down with the nervousness of a barometer during a September equinox, Granny represented security, stability, and assurance.

The stability was to be found in her cozy little sitting

room in Sandmere Road with its crocheted antimacassars on the chairs and the embroidered lambrequin draped along the mantelshelf. A pair of china Staffordshire dogs—white with red splotches—stood guard on either side of the over-mantel mirror.

The large gilt-framed engraving hanging above the horse-hair sofa, showing Queen Victoria and the Prince Consort surrounded by their progeny, was flanked by a similarly framed engraving of King Edward and Queen Alexandra. All my life, since those early days in Granny's sitting room, I have looked upon Queen Victoria as a most extraordinary woman; one who apparently, without the aid of hatpins or elastic, could balance a small, teetery crown on top of her smoothly brushed head at the same time as she dandled an obese infant on her satin-draped knee.

Granny was a mine of information concerning the Royal Family. Their births, marriages, coronations, widowings, and deaths provided her with constant and unlimited romance and drama. The British Royal Family belonged to her, as if they were a very superior family of paper dolls. Whenever I went to see Granny, I would ask her about the different members of the Royal Family, and she would tell me, confidentially, all the latest goings-on. I was under the impression that Granny was very much in the know about whatever happened at Buckingham Palace, Windsor, or Sandringham which was summed up in the impressive words "at Court."

A Bible and a worn black leather Book of Common Prayer were always on the little table beside Granny's bed in her bedroom, where everything smelled of Pears' Soap and lavender water. These represented the second article of Granny's faith; for if article one of her simple creed was her trust in the Crown, article two was her unquestioned faith in the Church of England.

Granny's respect for these two institutions was founded upon her equally categorical respect for herself and her class. So long as she did her duty toward her King on high and toward her King here below, she had every right to expect State and Church to do their duty toward her. There was no subservience in Granny's attitude toward king or bishop. She simply paid them the respect due the dignity of their positions, and in return she expected the State to give her security in this life, and the Church to usher her into a seat on the right hand of the Lord in the next.

Frequently on Sunday evenings I would go to church with her, carrying her prayerbook and finding the hymns from the numerals put up on the hymn boards beside the chancel. Granny and I shared the hymnbook, and our voices —hers still sweet, but a little husky and sometimes off key, mine higher, steadier, and a complete imitation of the boys' in the choir—would unite in the hymns and psalms which we both enjoyed immensely.

Many of the hymns were puzzling to me, and not a few of them seemed rather nasty with their references to sweat, wounds, and blood. How amazing that Granny, who had very strict ideas about what was and what was not nice, could still warble piously:

> *"There is a place where Jesus sheds*
> *The oil of gladness on our heads;*
> *A place than all besides more sweet:*
> *It is the blood-bought mercy seat."*

Religion, I thought, was certainly a very rum business. Take the word "bloody," for instance. What made this word quite proper in church and unforgivable in ordinary conversation?

Sometimes when Granny's rheumatism got the better of her piety, she would send me to church as her representative. Then I would be entrusted with the prayerbook and a sixpence for the offertory, tucked into the palm of my white cotton glove.

When I returned, Granny would ask expectantly: "Well, my dear, what was the sermon like? And what was the text?"

Following this lead, I would turn a chair around to form a pulpit and proceed to deliver a digest of the vicar's remarks for her appreciation. Of course it was necessary to dress up for this in Grandfather's coat and one of his collars, both worn back to front to give me a clerical look.

I must say I think I did the part of the reverend gentleman rather well, though I improved on his gestures and dramatized his style of delivery. Keeping in character, I would sing the hymns for Granny—not always those which we had sung at the service, but others which were my favorites.

After service Granny and I would have a cup of tea, and then, feeling relaxed and ready for a bit of amusement after all this edification, she would encourage me to sing for her songs she had taught me: "The Man Who Broke the Bank at Monte Carlo," "She's Only a Bird in a Gilded Cage," and "Champagne Charlie Is Me Name." For this act Grandfather's coat and collar were readjusted, his bowler hat and walking stick were produced, and the show was on.

Granny's frankly expressed preference was for little girls who were plump and rosy-cheeked. Tall, thin, sallow children looked half starved to her, and, therefore, she worried over my natural gawkiness.

"The child needs fattening up, Alice. Look at her. She's all legs."

"She's growing fast, Mother. I have to keep letting down the hems of her dresses until there is no more stuff to let out."

Granny sniffed. "It's the Danish blood, I expect. The Danish princes are all over six feet. And Her Majesty is extremely tall; though a fine figure of a woman, of course."

I preened to this. "Her Majesty" meant Queen Alexandra. I felt I had a special share in Her Majesty, who had come from Denmark, my father's country, and after whom I had been named.

Granny's next remark, however, dashed my self-esteem. "She's sallow too. I never did like a puny child. Some Scott's Emulsion would do her good. Mark my words, Alice, you'd do well to get a bottle and give her a spoonful night and morning."

"Very well, Mother. If you think so."

I loathed Scott's Emulsion, I gagged over each spoonful of the beastly stuff; but I knew better than to rebel. I had heard Granny's orders. So I was brought up on Scott's Emulsion to fatten me up, camphorated oil for my constant chest colds, and Parrish's Chemical Food, which was supposed to be a tonic. But I was no advertisement for all or any of these remedies, and Granny would sigh:

"Well, Gertie, I suppose you are just one of Pharaoh's lean kine."

Out of love, she made it sound like a compliment. Not to worry her, I submitted to Mother's habit of pinching my cheeks to make them look rosy whenever we approached Granny's doorstep. I even resorted to the trick of pinching my own cheeks when alone on her doorstep, waiting for her to let me in.

The popular taste was still for buxom beauties. His Majesty King Edward could 'ave 'is Jersey Lily; the British workingman preferred a nice generous armful.

The winter I was ten, and at a time when our finances hit rock bottom, Mother got herself a job in the chorus in a Christmas production of *Babes in the Wood* at the Brixton Theatre. The casting director studied her pleasing curves, listened to her voice, which was a very good soprano, and for once did not ask her to lift her long skirts to show her legs. This was fortunate, for though Mother had pretty ankles, the rest of her below the waist seemed to have no relation to the part of her above the waist. However, she had no false notions about her shape, and she had a very practical mind.

Having signed the contract, she came home with the flesh-colored tights supplied by the wardrobe mistress. Putting them on, she instructed me how to pad the legs of this garment with cotton wool to give her the much-desired and seductively rounded thighs which she unfortunately lacked. Of course it was possible to buy tights thus treated. These were called symmetricals. But they were very expensive, consequently necessity drove us to make ours at home.

Mother would stand on a chair in front of a mirror and direct me as I poked the wads of cotton down inside the silk tights. It was a long and tedious job, because the padding had to be sewn in smoothly so that it would not be detected.

Though I was only ten, I understood very clearly that her job in the chorus and the thirty shillings she was to get each week meant bread and groceries and coal and gaslight for us at home. I was well aware that it was up to me to make those legs satisfy the theater patrons and the eagle eye of the manager.

That is how I learned at a still tender age that frequently a woman's legs (and not her face) are her fortune.

3

FINALLY, after a week of waiting and rehearsals, our unit got its orders to leave for Hampshire.

There were eighteen of us, and we traveled in three cars —one large bus, one van for equipment, and a car for Mary, Stanley Kilbourn, my pianist, and me, with our driver.

Our first concert was aboard H.M.S. *Collingwood*. We had a great crowd—about thirty-five hundred enlisted personnel, WRENS, officers, the commodore, and his wife.

During my week of waiting in London I had been required to submit to the official censor the songs I had brought over from America to sing to the boys. Two of the songs were rated "not quite suitable for the B.B.C.," but they were finally passed as O.K. for the servicemen.

The songs I worked over and which I sang at that first concert were "A Lovely Way to Spend an Evening," which was one of Frank Sinatra's successes; Gertrude Niesen's song "I Wanna Get Married" from *Follow the Girls,* and "A Guy Named Joe." I also had the saga of an air-raid-shelter romance, entitled " 'E Vanished When the All-Clear Came." The last two numbers were written especially for me by two American boys, Bus Davis and Jim Carhart.

The most delightful surprise of the concert aboard H.M.S.

Collingwood was finding Richard seated in the front row. He had got leave for a couple of hours. There wasn't even time enough for him to take me back to the hotel in Portsmouth where Mary Barrett and I had been billeted; he had to return to his base. But even that glimpse of him was wonderful. It set me up no end.

I had just got into bed and was feeling terribly grateful for it after a long, hot, tiring, but exciting day.

"Good night, Mary. Have a nice, long, restful night."

"Good night," came Mary's voice from the other room, and, almost like a punctuation to that response, the sudden shriek of the sirens.

They were coming.

I sat up in bed in the dark and waited for the sound of the guns which would tell us the Germans were overhead. I shivered—not, I hoped, from fear, but from the suspense of waiting. I was under no misapprehension as to the amount of damage the raiders had done and could do to a town like Portsmouth. I had seen it with my own eyes.

Presently the guns started. It was strange to sit there in bed in the midst of my first real war experience. Between the enemy bombs and our own guns Portsmouth was actually the front. Yet in the street below people were calmly walking to air-raid shelters. One man went by whistling: "I Dream of Jeanie with the Light Brown Hair."

The "all clear" came after about an hour, and I dropped off to sleep. The next thing I knew Mary Barrett was shaking me awake. The guns were going like mad again. We sat and waited. Nothing happened; so Mary curled up on the foot of my bed and we dozed off until all at once the rocket gun on the sea front went off. We both shot up and out of the bed, grabbed our personal papers, and prepared to dash to the A.R. shelter if the hotel people notified us to do so. We had been told the rocket guns were not fired unless the enemy was overhead and flying low. They are precision guns and fire directly on the target; but, although they are very powerful, they apparently haven't a very long range. The noise they made was incredible; as if Jerry were dropping blockbusters. I really thought we had been hit.

Mary had been through it all many times over, on all the war fronts. She said the thing to do was to stay there in the room unless someone came and yanked us out. The only one who did turn up was Stanley, who came running down the corridor to see if we were all right. Stanley had been bombed out of four different homes during the blitz, and, as he put it, he was "fed oop with it all."

They chased Jerry out to sea about 2:30 A.M., then the "all clear" sounded, and we went back to bed and to sleep.

Next day Richard rang up to find out how I felt about it all. Now I could speak as a war veteran and I told him rather loftily that it felt better than being three thousand miles away, getting the news over the radio, and wondering where and how *he* was.

I saw some of the night's damage that day and the next, during which our unit covered the entire Southampton area. There was a new and very nasty hole in the side of the building next to our hotel. We had been lucky.

Every noon we put on the show at a plane factory or a shipyard or in a hangar for the workers, and at night we gave concerts at the camps. At the Civic Theatre in Southampton we played to some four thousand men and women, representing all the Allied nations and all branches of the service, and from there we went on to give a show under canvas—and in the pouring rain—at Camp C. 22 for two thousand American and British Rangers.

The whole area was feeling the suspense of approaching D-Day. No one, of course, would, or could, say when that would be, but the bases and the men were being "sealed." Driving home from a secret concert at Broderick for Americans and British about to leave, we passed thousands of "ducks" all lined up along the road to Southampton, ready to pull out at dawn for somewhere.

At the end of the show at C. 22, our manager, Norman Adams, called me aside and told me orders had just come through that our unit was to return to London immediately. In fact, he said, our show that night, which had gone particularly well, had almost been canceled in the middle of the bill. It seems that word had come through that the entire post was to be "sealed" and all E.N.S.A. units would have to evacuate or be sealed in until after D-Day for security reasons.

After swearing me to secrecy, Adams collected the whole unit and led us all to the officers' mess for refreshments. The mess was just a tent with a trestle table, but they put on quite a good meal for us, and the refreshment was good old bathtub gin with the kick of a bronco. As we laughed and joked, I wondered whether the men knew that I knew this was to be their last party for a long, long time. No mention was made of their departure, but as they crowded around our cars and shouted and waved to us as we drove away into the darkness back to London, I had the horrid feeling we were deserting them.

On arriving in London we were immediately re-routed to another coastal area. It turned out to be Brighton.

My orders came through to be ready to start on the morning of June 5. After leaving the Savoy, we drove through the districts of London that were home to me as a child—past Kennington Oval, past the "Horns Hotel" where my father had sung at smoking concerts for a guinea a night, past the Brixton Theatre where I made my stage debut at the age of ten for the magnificent sum of six shillings per week in that same Christmas play in which Mother had worn her homemade symmetricals.

The manager wanted a child who could sing and dance with nine others in a troupe, and one who could be trusted to be on time for the show and not get into mischief. Mother promised she would take care of all that, and I was taken on.

We children were little robin redbreasts in the forest ballet when the "Babes" got lost in the wood. Dressed in brown tights, very wrinkled at the knees, our skinny bodies clad in musty feathers and with hats which had beaks in front, we covered the two unfortunate children with artificial leaves to keep them from the cold until they were rescued by Robin Hood and his Merry Men. Mother was one of the Merry Men! I can remember to this day the song which Robin Hood sang in this scene. The chorus went like this:

There's a little green patch at the top of the hill,
Climb, boys, climb.
And it's there we can rest at our pleasure and will
Climb, boys, climb.
Though the way be dreary and your heart be weary,
It will all come right in time.

There's a little green patch at the top of the hill,
So climb, boys, climb.

This was sung with great gusto, accompanied by the marching up and down and suitable gestures and hearty thigh
slappings of Mother and the seven other Merry Men.

At this time Mother had a friend, who was a friend of
the mother of Ivy Shilling who played Alice when Lewis
Carroll's immortal story was dramatized for a Christmas
production. I was taken to see the play. We sat in a box,
which was the first time in my life I ever enjoyed such
prominence. I watched every move, every gesture of Alice's,
and my envy of Ivy Shilling gave me no rest until I nagged
Mother into taking me to Miss Conti's dancing school, at
which she was a pupil.

Miss Italia Conti held a unique place in the world of the
British theater. She had a basement studio just off Great
Portland Street where the boys and girls she accepted as
pupils practiced dance steps, did acrobatic exercises on the
horizontal bar, and were taught elocution and the rudi-
ments of the drama. The studio was a big room lined with
mirrors in which you could see yourself from every angle,
and at one end was a small stage with a piano.

Mother had no money to pay for dancing and singing
lessons for me. Dad had suffered a run of bad luck for
months, and we had moved to cheaper and still cheaper
lodgings. My education did not benefit by these flittings
about Clapham and Brixton; whenever we moved into a
new district it usually meant my entering a new school. It
also meant finding myself one of a new group of children,
who stood off and eyed me suspiciously.

The boys and girls at Miss Conti's eyed each other too. But their glances were different. They looked at me critically, but not at my clothes or where I lived, but for what I was able to do. Many of them had been born into theatrical families. All of them aspired to stardom.

I sang and danced for Miss Conti, and she thought me sufficiently talented to offer to give me free lessons. On these terms I was enrolled one afternoon a week for a six weeks' trial period. If I showed promise, I had the opportunity of staying on as a pupil-teacher, thereby repaying my tuition.

I am a little hazy about those weeks at Miss Conti's. It was an entirely new world to me. I am under the impression that Noel Coward was already a pupil there when I started. If he was not, he came very soon after, because Noel figures largely in all my memories of Miss Conti. Anton Dolin joined the school later to study Shakespeare.

Noel was a thin, unusually shy boy with a slight lisp. He was studying elocution, acting, and dancing (or should I say deportment?) and was one of Miss Conti's star pupils. Noel's people were in a position to give him educational advantages. They were "comfortably situated."

Noel wasn't snobbish about this; in fact, he and I, who were about the same age, entered at once into an alliance.

This doesn't mean that Noel wasn't occasionally condescending to me, but this condescension sprang from a quite natural masculine impulse to put in her place an irrepressible and very plain-looking small girl who had the annoying faculty of getting herself noticed. I could put up with the condescension. What I could not have endured was to have Noel ignore me.

However, even at the age of eleven I suffered no illusions as to what constituted the charm I had for Noel Coward. I was the proud possessor of a bicycle, bought for me from the boy next door by a friend of Dad's. The bicycle originally had a bar across the middle, but Mother, ever practical, paid a man to saw this off so a girl could ride it. However, even she could not alter the drooping handlebars which showed it was a boy's model. Noel pointed this out immediately:

"It's quite unsuitable for a girl."

He could not conceal from me the fact that he wanted a bicycle, which was something his family would not permit him to have.

But Noel had a possession which I secretly coveted—a phonograph with a large spreading horn. He also owned a stack of records. So we made a deal. He could ride my bicycle in return for lending me his phonograph for the same length of time. I imagine that sort of lend-lease is as good a basis for a lifelong friendship as any other.

Noel's records greatly increased my acquaintance with the popular music of the day. They also brought me the beauty of "The Blue Danube," the sweet rhythm of "Valse Triste," and the sticky romance of the "Indian Love Lyrics."

So once a week I packed my small attaché case containing my toe-dancing slippers, my practice clothes, soap and a towel, and took the bus to Great Portland Street, always in the hope that Noel would be there.

Miss Conti had undertaken to teach me to dance and to sing, at least to the extent of fitting me to appear in one of the Christmas plays. These are a part of the holiday season in England, and the theater managers always went to Miss Conti for child actors to play in them. Miss Conti found no fault either with my leg work or my vocal efforts. But my accent, which was pure cockney, caused her to wince. One day she led me to the piano and, after laying a sheet of paper under the strings, she struck a chord.

"That, my dear Gertrude," she said, "is what your voice sounds like to me."

My quick ear recognized the similarity between the tinny vibrations and my own accent. That was my introduction to phonetics.

I was not yet good enough to appear in one of the London Christmas plays. However, I was approved for a part in a fairy play called *Fifinella*, which was put on at the Repertory Theatre in Liverpool. We were rehearsed in London, under Miss Conti's careful eye, and then sent up in the care of a matron and her husband, Mr. and Mrs. Murray. Estelle Winwood played the beautiful Fairy Queen, but she made little impression on me because I had eyes only for the Prince in his scarlet tights and doublet. This fascinating hero was played by Eric Blore. And it was obvious that no one had found it necessary to pad *his* tights with cotton wool.

The first time Noel and I appeared together was in a German morality play, *Hannela*, put on at Manchester, under the direction of Mr. Basil Dean. Noel and I played angels in white robes, gilded wings, and sanctimonious smiles. Neither of us, as I remember, cared for the play or for our parts in it. However, we touched the heart of Noel's kindly uncle, for he asked permission to take us for an afternoon's outing.

It was Christmas week, and the shops were full of entrancing things to buy. By various ruses Noel and I enticed him to one shopwindow after the other, artfully pointing out what each of us would like to receive for a Christmas present. But our benefactor was not in a generous mood that day. Not till the afternoon was nearly over did he weaken and buy us a large box of peppermint creams, which he made us promise to divide with the other children in the cast.

Noel and I managed to forget this admonition and to eat most of the sweets ourselves in the taxi on the way home. Soon I began to feel very queer. When we went on in the heaven scene, the other celestial beings seemed to float and bob dizzily around me. I stole a glance at Noel. He was positively green. Presently the audience was permitted an unexpected vision of heaven in which two small angels were being violently sick.

I couldn't have been a total failure as an angel, because soon after *Hannela* I was given a job in *The Miracle* then being put on by Reinhardt at the Olympia. The play called for one hundred children—fifty boys and fifty girls. As we did two shows a day, and the children came from homes all over London, the London County Council established a special school for us at Olympia. We had classes in the mornings, then dinner, after which it was time to dress and be made up for the daily matinee. Olympia is out beyond Shepherd's Bush, a wearying, long tram ride home after the evening performance.

It must have been that summer that Dad took Mother and me on a Sunday excursion to Brighton. The resort was crowded with trippers like ourselves; the bands kept up a ceaseless accompaniment of music, and the Pierrot troupes on the sands played to enormous business. I watched their performance with a critical eye; after all, I was now in the profession.

On the pier, among other penny-in-the-slot machines was one showing a gaudily painted picture of a gypsy. The machine promised to tell your fortune for a penny. I dropped my copper piece into the slot and waited anxiously while the machine ground out a few bars of a popular tune; it then proceeded to stick a tongue of pink cardboard at me. There were words printed on it. I tore off the slip and read my penny destiny:

> *A star danced,*
> *And you were born.*

I accepted my fate without hesitation. The gypsy meant to tell me that I would be a dancer and someday I would be a star.

A few days later I stopped in at the printers in Clapham High Street and ordered some cards made. I had written out what I wished the printer to put on these bits of pasteboard:

LITTLE GERTIE LAWRENCE

Child Actress and Danseuse

BRIXTON THEATRE

I had used the name Lawrence, because that was the stage name Mother used. I was especially proud of the word "danseuse," which, according to the old gentleman who printed the cards, meant "dancer" in French. Already I could see my name in electric lights on Shaftesbury Avenue. I had never been to that thoroughfare except on a bus, but I had heard about it and dreamed of it as children today talk and dream about Hollywood.

I did not show the pink slip of paper with my fortune to anyone; perhaps I was afraid it would not come true if I shared the secret. But my professional cards were different. I scattered them like confetti and with complete self-assurance.

The mother of "your cousin Ruby," who up to now had produced the most promising child in the family, said to Mother: "Do you want your child in that sort of life, Alice? I wouldn't. Not for my Ruby."

"Your Ruby hasn't the temperament," Mother countered. "You've got to have temperament for the stage."

"Temperament! Well, Alice, you can call it that if you like. Myself, I'd give a plainer name to it. And when it comes to temperament, anyone would think you'd had enough of that with Gertie's father. If she was *my* child and had his blood in her veins, I wouldn't let her near a theater. That I wouldn't."

Cousin Ruby's mother had maneuvered Mother into an impossible situation. She could not defend my father without appearing disloyal to Dad, or without drawing down on her the obvious retort: "Well, if he was as good as all that, why did you ever leave him?"

It may have been such conversations as these with my aunt which unlocked my Mother's reticence. Up until then she had never mentioned my father to me.

We were out shopping one day when suddenly she stopped to read a playbill stuck up on a wall. It advertised a minstrel show. Heading the cast as the star appeared the name: "Arthur Lawrence."

"That's your father, Gertie," said Mother, pointing.

I stared at the name, trying to accustom myself to the idea of a relationship between this man and me. No one had ever told me much about my father. I could not remember having seen him or heard of his taking the slightest interest in my existence. Dad was all the father I had known, or needed. This strange man on the playbill seemed suddenly to trespass on Dad's position. I slid a questioning glance at Mother. She was still staring at the poster. Her voice was suddenly wistful—and a little proud: "Well, now you know. He's a fine singer. You get your talent from him."

We walked on, and no more was said about my father. I would have liked to have gone to the theater to see him and hear him sing, but Mother did not suggest it. I only had to look at her to realize that the subject was closed. But the sudden discovery that I had a father who was a success in the theater set me thinking.

I was now nearly thirteen. For several years I had been appearing in plays from time to time, earning a few shillings a week. The gypsy had given assurance that my fortune lay in the theater. As I compared Dad—dear, lovable, but unsuccessful—with my own father, whose name appeared in big letters on the playbill, a plan began to develop in my mind. I began to watch the bookings of the minstrel show starring Arthur Lawrence.

For all that I might not have done anything about it except for two things which happened simultaneously. We were undergoing one of our periodic lean periods. These seemed to occur more frequently and lasted longer as Dad's luck became more and more elusive. And of necessity I had been taken away from Miss Conti's.

One evening several months later, when Mother and Dad were out, I decided to carry out my plan, and I packed a few belongings in a small straw portmanteau. I then collected all the empty bottles and jars in the house, returned them to the grocer's, and got the money I needed for the journey. Wearing my best coat and a large mushroom-shaped hat, and carrying the portmanteau, I took the tram to the theater where I knew my father was appearing. A note left on the kitchen table for Mother and Dad told them of my decision to join my father, and that they were not to worry.

The stage doorman looked at me suspiciously. "Now then, what do you want, youngster?" he demanded.

"I've come to see Mr. Lawrence."

He frowned. "It's not at all likely Mr. Lawrence will see you. He's dressing now to go on."

"I'll wait," I said, and set down the portmanteau. "It's very important."

Perhaps something in my tone made the doorman realize that this was no ordinary occasion. He squinted at me sharply.

"What's your name? I'll tell Mr. Lawrence you're here."

I swallowed. "Just tell him it's Gertie."

The doorman went away, slamming the door to prevent my slipping in. For a moment I felt an impulse to turn and run. There was still time to return to Clapham—to seize and destroy the penciled note I had left letting Mother and Dad know my decision. But something—my own destiny perhaps —held me there on the bench inside the stage door. Presently I heard steps coming along the corridor and a mutter of voices. The door opened . . .

A man stood there—a very tall man who leaned forward to peer down at me in the dim, flickering light of the gas bracket in its wire cage. He was in his shirt sleeves and collarless. One half of his face was smeared with grease and burnt cork. Out of the black face a pair of very blue eyes stared at me in utter incredulity. He spoke in a deep, quiet voice:

"Who are you? What are you doing here?"

I drew my card from my pocket and handed it to him. His eyes took in the printed words, then came back to me.

"I'm Gertie," I said. "And I've come to stay."

4

Driving down to Brighton on that June day, strangely it was the memories of the past which were more vivid and more alive in my mind than the scenes we drove through. That glimpse of Kennington Oval and Brixton brought back events and persons I had not thought of in years. For some reason or other, and I suppose only a psychologist could explain it, this visit home to a fighting England was like a visit to a psychoanalyst. In *Lady in the Dark* I had played the part of a successful businesswoman who had been psychoanalyzed. Her dreams were reproduced on the stage in fantastic scenes. In somewhat the same way, recollections of "Little Gertie Lawrence—child actress and danseuse," began to form scenes that were scarcely less fantastic than those imagined by Moss Hart for *Lady in the Dark*.

Suddenly I smelled again the cold, dusty, tremendously exciting smell of backstage in that Music Hall Theatre when Father, still holding my card in one hand, reached out the other and caught me by the wrist. He pulled me over the threshold, past the doorman, and let the stage door slam behind us.

"Come along to my dressing room. Curtain's going up in five minutes. I've got to finish dressing. You can wait there. I'll talk to you later on. Sit down. And for God's sake, don't cry."

I had begun to weep from relief, fear, and the physical reaction to the whole adventure.

In the dressing room stood a woman holding the coat Father was to put on. He paid no attention to her, but went on rapidly blacking the rest of his face before the mirror. After which he put on a curly black wig and stuck it down with spirit gum.

"She's Gertie," he said out of the grotesque red mouth he had quickly painted in the middle of the black face. "She's my kid, Rose."

Rose did not move. She looked at me not unkindly and I stared back at her. I was not prepared for Rose.

A callboy went along the corridor calling, "Mr. Lawrence, please!"

Father turned from the mirror, his make-up completed, and thrust his arms into the evening coat Rose silently held out for him. He jerked down his waistcoat, twitched his white tie a fraction of an inch, and was gone.

Only then Rose turned to me, standing there gripping my portmanteau and staring. "So you're Arthur's little girl," she said. "How old are you?"

"I'm thirteen," I said.

"You are! Well . . ." She looked me over appraisingly. "There's not much of you."

Rose herself was what Granny would have called a fine figure of a woman, which meant she had plenty of curves. She had also, I noticed, very pretty ankles. Show girl, I thought.

Rose told me I had better sit down because we would have a long wait. A minstrel show wasn't like a play in which the actors frequently left the stage for long periods.

Once the curtain was up, my father would remain on stage until the end of the act.

During that wait Rose and I became acquainted. She had a kind heart and there was no guile in her. She loved my father and said so with a disarming frankness. She continued to tidy up the dressing room. "We've been together six years, Arthur and me. That's more than a lot of married couples can say. Oh, not but what we've had our quarrels. And who hasn't, I'd like to know."

I nodded. I found myself liking Rose, who admitted me so hospitably into the intimacy of her life. But it was clear that she did not intend to consider me one of the family.

"You can't stay with us," she went on. "You know that, I suppose?" (I didn't. How could I, when I had never known of the existence of Rose until that evening?)

Then she said: "Your mother will be here to fetch you back tonight or in the morning, and there'll be all hell to pay."

I told her I had left a note for Mother and that I couldn't go back. But immediately Rose dashed my plans by remarking: "Well, you can't stay on with Arthur and me. We can't travel you."

Strangely, that possibility had not occurred to me. I began to wish I had not left the note. Still, I thought, something might happen to prevent Mother coming tonight. Meanwhile, I had to win Rose over to my side. I told her about my experience as an actress, emphasizing the fact that Miss Conti considered I had talent. I showed Rose my card.

She was obviously impressed.

"How nice! Danseuse looks elegant. Quite West End."

"I think so," I agreed complacently.

When Father came off stage, he found us chatting comfortably. Perhaps this lifted a worry from his mind.

"The kid's all right, Arthur," Rose said. "She's got a lot of you in her, I'd say." She repeated to him briefly what I had told her about my experience in the theater. "She must be good."

Was it Rose's acceptance of me which persuaded my father to keep me with him? I have sometimes thought so. That, and a curious pride in the child who had followed his profession, made my father suddenly laugh and say to me: "You can stay with us for tonight, anyway. We'll find a place for you somewhere in our digs. She can sleep on the sofa, can't she, Rose? We'll send a telegram to your mother this minute and tell her you're all right. Tomorrow we can talk things over."

Mother did not appear until the next morning. What passed between my parents I never knew, but an arrangement was made by which I was to remain with Father as long as I wished to do so and he would support me. I was to write to Mother once a week and keep her informed of my whereabouts. If anything went wrong, she was to be immediately advised of it and was to come and take me back to live with her.

That is how my life with Father and Rose began. I shared their lodgings and whatever they had. Whatever I earned. when I had a job, Father got, under our joint contract, since I was under age.

Although I missed Mother and Dad terribly, I missed Granny even more. I often thought of her and her tidy little house. I missed the news of the Royal Family. King Edward VII had died—his funeral was the first state pageant I had not read about in history books. Now all the talk was of the coronation of King George V and Queen Mary. To me, as to millions of children throughout the Empire, the leading personage at the forthcoming coronation was the youthful Prince of Wales. Perhaps our generation derived an immense amount of satisfaction from the fact that one of us was to occupy a prominent place at the Abbey ceremony. The newspapers and illustrated weeklies were full of photographs of H.R.H. Prince Edward and his sister and brothers. The princess interested me very little, but every photograph of Prince Edward I came across I cut out and pinned to the wall of my room. The increasing collection of photographs traveled with me.

And we were constantly on the move, touring the Midlands, swinging back to London to look for fresh engagements. When we were not working, I amused myself in any way that I could. I did the shopping for Rose and helped her keep our lodgings tidy. We made our own clothes, trimmed our own hats. I made myself a hobble skirt out of a remnant of tweed when I was fourteen. Rose appreciated these efforts of mine. She was not a housekeeper, but she was neat, and Father's untidiness was a constant annoyance to her.

Life wasn't all beer and skittles. Not by any means. Father still liked his glass, and though he would go several months without drinking, invariably there came a day when he would become short-tempered, restless, and start going out between the matinee and the night show. Finally he would crack up. Then he became ugly, cruel, and impossible to handle. Neither Rose nor I could do anything with him.

I began to watch for these drinking bouts and to dread

them and the rows that went on at the theater with the manager and other members of the company and at home with Rose. In between spells Rose and I formed a conspiracy to keep Father in bounds. One or the other of us kept watch over him all the time. We would try to think up schemes for keeping him happy and entertained, but when our cleverness failed to win over Father's craving, Rose and I knew we were in for it. Father would go on drinking, growing more and more sullen, more and more difficult to handle, until the manager paid us off. Since Father and I were always on a joint contract, this meant I lost my job when he was fired. When that happened, he would drink himself into a state in which he was unable to go out at all. Poor Rose then put him to bed and nursed him until he sobered. Father would emerge from her hands chastened, and go out to hunt a new engagement for himself and for me. We had no agent. We could not afford an agent's commission. It was our habit to search the "Wanted" ads in the theatrical newspapers. Sometimes Father heard of something through hanging around the crowds by the London Hippodrome.

We had been out of work for several weeks and were more than usually hard up when Father landed a job to play in a touring revival of André Messager's *The Little Michus*, a comic operetta for which his voice was perfect. He came home to the dreary back room in Camberwell where he and I were then living to tell me the good news. Rose was away on tour with a concert party. That room which was divided into two private apartments by a curtain suspended from a sagging wire represented the ebb tide of our fortunes.

But Father beamed over his good luck. He planked down

a couple of half crowns from the advance he had persuaded the company manager to give him and said gaily:

"Let's have sausages for supper, Gertie. This calls for a celebration, my girl."

I pocketed the coins and made ready to go out and do the shopping. Meanwhile Father ran on about the company and the play. He was to play M. Michu, the proprietor of a patisserie and the perplexed parent of twin daughters, Marie Blanche and Blanche Marie—the "little Michus." Immediately I pricked up my ears.

"Who will play the girls?" I demanded.

"Not a chance of it," Father smiled at me ruefully. "I spoke to the manager about you. He was interested until he asked me your age, and I had to tell him fifteen. Then he wouldn't hear of it. He insists he must have someone older. It's too bad, because you could do it, I'm sure."

I thought hard. I went to the mirror and studied what I saw there. What could I do to myself to add three or four years to my age?

"Are you sure he hasn't filled both parts yet?"

Father said he was. "He has one girl. She's about your height. But she's nineteen or twenty, I'd say."

My hair was long and hung in curls to my waist. I brushed out the ringlets and for the first time put my hair up. I rummaged in the cupboard and brought out my one straw hat. I cut off the brim, pinned on a bunch of cherries, and contrived a toque which could be called anything but youthful. In my tweed hobble skirt I looked at least eighteen.

Thus arrayed, and with Father's encouragement, I presented myself at the manager's office and asked for the job.

He tried my voice and engaged me on a joint contract with Father, as I was still under age, no matter how old I looked.

Father and I toured with *The Little Michus* for many weeks. When Rose's engagement ran out, she joined us. We were playing to good business and it looked as though the show would have a long run. Then Father succumbed to one of his drinking spells. Rose and I did our best to straighten him out and to cover him up. But as the drinking went on for days, the manager fired him.

This meant that I, too, was once more out of work.

"I'd like to keep you on, kid," the manager said regretfully. "You're good. But you're under age, and what can I do?"

Rose took Father in hand once more and I searched the columns of notices in *The Stage* for a new job. This time I intended to lie boldly about my age. Rose agreed with me it was the thing to do. "It's no life for you, being with Arthur," she said. "He's hopeless. I know that now. You must go on your own. You've got something, Gertie. I think you're going to get on. You're not pretty and you're too thin for everybody's taste, but you've got *class*. You know, I wouldn't be surprised if you were up in the West End one of these days."

"Oh, Rose. Do you really think so?"

Rose nodded solemnly. "Yes, I do. You've got something that goes down with a certain kind of audience. High-toned. It's just that you've got to be seen by the right people. And that takes some doing."

"I'll land something before long," I assured her.

What I landed was a job as chorus girl and understudy in a traveling revue—one of the first of its kind—entitled

Miss Plaster of Paris. I had been forced to lie about my age, but we needed the money desperately. The man who ran the show and his wife played the leading parts. I worked in the chorus, played maids, and in one scene sat on a column. I was selected for this honor because mine was the smallest posterior in the company.

All week I looked forward to Saturday night when "the ghost walked" and we were paid. Pay night usually meant a good spree for the manager followed by a fight with his wife in the course of which he frequently gave her a black eye, thus paving the way to my appearance in the leading role the following Monday. For all this excitement and experience I received fifteen shillings a week.

I managed very well on this sum. Three or four of us lived together, sharing room rent and pooling our money for the catering purse. We took turns doing the marketing each day. It was a hard-and-fast rule that we count the potatoes before giving them to the landlady to cook for us. She was under orders to boil, not to mash them. This enabled us to be sure she had not helped herself to a couple of them. Sometimes one of us would forget to give the order, and when the vegetable dish cover was lifted, a groan would go up:

"Oh, blast! The old bitch has mashed 'em!"

The manager had an old white bull terrier which traveled with the show. The bulldog had appeared with his master when he played Bill Sykes. At rehearsal one day, when we were back in London preparing a second revue called *Miss Lamb of Canterbury*, I was playing with the dog when he suddenly growled and sank his teeth into my right hand, refusing to let go.

I fainted. A doctor was sent for. I was cauterized, bandaged, and told to go home. I was living in lodgings with Father. Rose had finally left him, "and this time for good," she had asserted. "Enough is enough, but too much is a little bit too much, if you ask me. And that's what I've had with Arthur. Oh, I've walked out on him before to teach him a lesson. And every time he's come round within the fortnight and made all sorts of promises, and I've listened to him and gone back. I can't say I've ever taught him a thing except what a man like him knows already--that a woman like me can be an awful fool. This time, though, I don't care about teaching Arthur anything. It's myself I'm thinking about. And high time too. Myself and you, Gertie."

"Me?"

"Yes, you. Because, don't you see if I stay on with your father you probably will too. And what would happen then? I've been seeing it coming for the last year. You and I would be working and keeping him. The way it is, if Arthur wants to eat and drink, he's got to work. And that means he'll keep sober more or less. Without him, you've got no one but yourself to think about. This is your chance to get ahead."

There was something in what Rose said. I thought it over and decided I should stand on my own. Father had been out of work for some time, but that morning he had told me he had a chance to go to South Africa. This seemed too good to be true. On the way home a thought struck me: if he knows what has happened to my hand he may refuse to go so far away. "He must go. He must," I kept saying all the way home.

Father was there when I arrived. He was tremendously

excited. He had only to sign his contract next day and he would leave in a week.

"You will be all right, won't you, Gertie?" he said eagerly. "You are getting on fine, and this will be a great chance for me to earn some decent money and see a bit of the world. South Africa is a great country. A man can start life over again out there."

I assured him I was at the top of my form, and kept my bandaged hand behind me, saying nothing of the intense pain. When he finally noticed the bandage I explained I had cut my hand on a broken glass at rehearsal. Father never knew the truth about my injury, which took a long time to heal and left a scar which is still visible. He went off to South Africa and I managed to keep working. He was gone about a year. He came home well and bronzed and self-assured. When I met him at the boat, he introduced me to an enormous, handsome man with whom he had made friends during his trip. This was Victor McLaglen.

Unfortunately South Africa had not made Father's fortune or changed his habits. But something had changed in me during the months he was away. I had learned to stand alone, and by managing to keep on tour I never lived with Father again. He retired to Brighton, did an occasional show or a concert, and later on I was able to help him until his death.

In between jobs I lived at the "Cats' Home" in London so that I could make the rounds of the theatrical managers' offices. This was a tall, gaunt house in Charlotte Street which called itself The Theatrical Girls' Boarding House. Here, for ten shillings a week, you could luxuriate in a cubicle by yourself. For five shillings you shared a room with another girl. For half a crown you could have a cot in a dormitory. I never reached the ten-shilling private-cubicle stage.

There was a great feeling of camaraderie at the Cats' Home. We girls loaned each other tram fares and clothes to look our best when seeking a job. There was a sewing room where we made our own clothes, and the stars of the London theaters used to send their discarded gowns to us to be raffled off at sixpence a ticket. I remember winning a pink net evening gown with a harem skirt and ornamented with beads. This I sent to Mother as a gift. She wrote saying it was beautiful and she was going to put it in a raffle! That pink net confection may still be going the rounds.

These and other memories filled the long, beautiful drive across Surrey and over the Sussex Downs, which I remembered so well from the days when I used to drive this way to Brighton to visit Pamela at her school, Roedean.

Odd to think of Pamela, my daughter, having any connection with the little girl who ran away to seek her fortune on the stage. The decade which separated that little girl from Pamela's mother was crowded with experiences. Four of those years were filled with World War I, toward the close of which Pamela was born. Long before I had the responsibility of a child I had entered upon another responsibility—one which had remained unfulfilled until I made this trip to England to entertain the Tommies and the G.I. Joes who were pledged to defend the way of life I want Pamela and all other children to have. I shall come to the story of that responsibility and how I entered upon it a little later.

All the gay Regency recklessness was gone from

Brighton. Barbed wire prevented access to the sea front. The old, well-tanned houses, which always used to remind me of Indian colonels basking in the sun, with their backs to the protecting downs, showed plenty of battle scars. But there was still the old, steady, carrying-on spirit at the Old Ship Hotel where our unit was billeted. In the old days, when I came to Brighton, I had a suite at the Albion or the Metropole, but these places had been taken over by the services, and only the Old Ship remained for civilians. I was grateful for my billet there—a single bedroom without a bath.

It was June 5 when we arrived in Brighton, and we did a show that night at Tilgate Camp, outside Crawley, in a Nissen hut.

The air in the hut, which was packed with soldiers, wedged shoulder to shoulder, seemed to quiver with anticipation. It was bound to be very soon now, almost any hour, that the United Nations would launch their long-prepared-for blow at the continent. The quivering you felt was like that of a boxer who draws back a second before lashing out with both fists at his opponent.

"Oh, it's a lovely way to spend an evening," I sang to the rows upon rows of faces that, from the stage, looked like spume on a khaki-colored sea. Silly words, and ironic under the circumstances. These words were on my lips, but while I sang them my heart was speaking those marvelous lines from *King Henry V*:

> *Now entertain conjecture of a time*
> *When creeping murmur and the poring dark*
> *Fills the wide vessel of the universe.*

From camp to camp through the foul womb of night
The hum of either army stilly sounds,
That the fix'd sentinels almost receive
The secret whispers of each other's watch:
Fire answers fire, and through their paly flames
Each battle sees the other's umber'd face;
Steed threatens steed, in high and boastful neighs
Piercing the night's dull ear; and from the tents
The armourers, accomplishing the knights,
With busy hammers closing rivets up,
Give dreadful note of preparation . . .

A country cock crowed, though it was not yet "the third hour of drowsy morning," when we tumbled out of the cars, before the door of the Old Ship, and stumbled up the stairs to bed.

How odd to begin a day so momentous as June 6, 1944, with tea and toast. A breeze which smelled like the wind which blows across the sand dunes at Dennis lifted my bedroom curtains and set me longing to go out for a bathe. Brighton was very quiet except for the recurrent waves of planes flying high overhead—that monotonous accompaniment to life in wartime England. The newspaper brought the news that Rome had been ours since the day before. All dwellers in the continental coast towns had been warned by the army commander in chief to evacuate their homes at once. A headline announced that His Majesty would speak on the air that night.

Were we on the eve of the invasion at last?

I went downstairs with my hands full of letters for the

post. It was the old hall porter, in his green baize apron, who told me that D-Day was at last a reality. Our forces had set sail during the night for Normandy. That tremor I had felt the night before was not imagined. I had caught the "dreadful note of preparation."

Mary Barrett and I walked out into the sunshine and along the Front. The people we met were very quiet and looked a little grim, conscious of what must be taking place only forty-four miles across the Channel. Whenever a bevy of planes passed overhead, pointing toward France, all eyes were lifted to them and, I dare say, all hearts. I know mine was. I wanted desperately to speak to Richard, but I was told all civilian telephone calls were canceled. I knew he must be in the midst of the busiest day for the Navy.

On the evening of D-Day our unit was scheduled to do a show on the pier at Worthing. The spirits of the men in the audience ran high, and no wonder, with good news coming in that our invading army had made an advance of ten miles into France within a few hours of landing. Worthing is only a few miles east of Bognor, where I had my first glimpse of the sea and where I earned my first sovereign. The Victorian poets had a fancy for writing odes to places "revisited." This tour of the south coast was full of such places for me.

The next day, Wednesday, the War Department unsealed a camp for us, and we motored out toward Lewes to Camp Tanner. The men had rigged up an old barn to serve as a crude theater. When we arrived there, we found the troops in the process of moving out for France. Hundreds had already left. From what one could learn, the invasion was going so well—"going according to plan" as Churchill announced to the Empire—and the advance into France was so swift that more men were being dispatched in a continuous stream.

The troops about to leave were already lined up when we arrived. They carried all their equipment and were wearing their Mae Wests. A groan went through the ranks because they thought they would miss our show.

So we unloaded fast, and the colonel (his name was Bury, and the outfit was called "Bury's Bashers") let them into the barn theater where we did our show for them. I sang my songs and then stood out in the farmyard waving to them as they drove out, headed for France.

It was all like part of a film. There I stood in the middle of that once-peaceful farmyard, in the brilliant sunshine, tears streaming down my face, waving good-by to those men—knowing I was the last woman to sing them a song for many a weary while.

When the trucks had pulled out, we returned to the barn and did our show again for the men who were still waiting for orders. Halfway through the bill we had to stop while the troops were summoned to muster outside. Again I went out, and kissed them and waved good-by. Again we struck up "Auld Lang Syne." Above the rumbling of the lorries rose the sound of men's voices singing the song which I had just taught them.

By this time Mary Barrett and I were both reduced to pulp. But the show had to go on; so, with an ache in my heart, I went back to the barn and we did a third show.

There was no one to know that what I was doing there that afternoon—and what I was to do for many days at many other camps throughout England—was the long-over-due payment of a debt. Bury's Bashers and the other boys I sang to could not know what I owed to half a dozen British Tommies of World War I who, before they went out to fight in Flanders, gave Gertrude Lawrence her chance to become a star.

5

Though I was now entirely on my own, without obligation to Father, I did not go back to Clapham. What held me back from doing this was bravado. I had left them and Granny to further my career as an actress. I was still a long way from achieving that goal and, therefore, I felt hesitant about going back to the family. Above all, I had no desire to have the virtues of Cousin Ruby dinned into my ears. Someday, I promised myself, I'll be doing so well I can afford to go back.

I was determined to make good, and deep inside myself was the unshaken conviction that I would be a success someday. I was quite willing to work for that success and to make sacrifices to attain it. I did work, not forgetting Miss Conti's teaching, and striving all the time to do better. Many of the girls I met in the companies in which I played, or at the Cats' Home, admitted, frankly, that they were content just to be good enough to get by, make a good marriage, and settle down. They, apparently, did not have that insistent, not-to-be-ignored inner drive which forced me to learn more and always more about the theater.

I cannot take any credit to myself for this determination to succeed, for it was inherent in my nature. I did have to battle through periods of despair and frustration. But I am by nature hopeful. I do not understand defeat. My own psychology in those years before I was seventeen was quite simple: I believed, unquestionably, that I was destined to be an actress. The fortune which the penny-in-the-slot machine on the pier at Brighton had given me seemed to me to state this quite unequivocally. I saw no reason to doubt the gypsy's prophecy. It might be this season—or the next— that I would emerge from the obscurity of the chorus of a musical which played the provinces and the cheaper suburbs of London. But emerge I would. Meanwhile it was up to me to make myself as good as I could be. Each performance was a fresh challenge.

One night after the show in Swindon there was a knock on the chorus's dressing-room door. The callboy handed me a card which read LEE WHITE AND CLAY SMITH, LONDON AND NEW YORK. I went out and found an American couple on vacation from their London season. They were visiting Swindon to see the cathedral and had dropped in at our show.

They took me out to supper at their hotel and we talked. "You're good," Lee said to me seriously. "You don't belong in a show like this. You've got something. Clay and I are going to keep our eyes on you." She made me promise to keep them informed of what towns we played, and let them know whenever I changed shows. "You never can tell," she finished; "we may learn of something. And, when we do, you'll hear from us."

I rather doubted the validity of this promise, but from time to time I would send them a picture post card to the address Lee gave me.

Nearly a year later, while I was playing in Yarmouth, I

received a telegram. It was signed *Lee White and Clay Smith*, and it said tersely that they had recommended me for a job in a revue which André Charlot was staging in London. *Can you come at once?* the wire ended.

I was all for dashing to the station and leaping aboard the first London Express, but the other girls, to whom I had shown the wire, held me back.

"How do you know this is a genuine offer?" they demanded. "Suppose you leave the show here and go flying up to London only to find the manager has signed someone else? There you'll be—out of a job and without a bean."

These suggestions sobered me. "What'll I do? I can't afford to throw over a chance like this, can I? It's for London!"

The girls agreed wholeheartedly that this was not to be thought of. We put our heads together and concocted a return message: *Does your wire constitute a contract?* I ran down to the P.O. and sent it off; then I went back to the theater to dress for that night's show, trying desperately to keep my mind on my cues and not on the extravagant fancies that kept popping up when I thought of London.

When I came off stage after the final curtain, the stage doorman handed me a telegram. I ripped it open. With the other girls crowding around, peering over my shoulder, I read:

YES, IF YOU CAN COME AT ONCE, THIS TELEGRAM
CONSTITUTES A CONTRACT. CLAY SMITH.

Luckily, I had no contract with the present show, but if I was to leave I had to do so without the management getting wind of it. Back in our lodgings, my roommate, Madge,

and I took stock of our resources. It was a Tuesday night—
four days to payday. What money I had plus all that she
could afford to lend me wouldn't pay for a third-class ticket
to London. Neither of us owned anything of value that we
could pawn. We looked at each other, and for the first time
in my life I felt desperate. Here was my chance—a chance
for a contract at a London theater, and for the lack of a
few shillings I couldn't seize it. Madge said slowly:

"I've got a friend in camp here. I'll get word to him. If he
has any money, he'll help us. And, if he hasn't, he'll know
how to raise it."

We didn't sleep much that night. I lay tense, staring into
the dark. Somehow, by some means or other, I must get the
money for that ticket to London. Next morning I was
packed and ready to take off when Madge went out to meet
her boy friend. She came back in a short time, bringing him
with her. He was a little, bright-faced lad from Bristol. Before he enlisted, he'd been a joiner's apprentice. Now he was
drilling with a regiment of gunners, getting ready to go
over to Flanders. Madge showed him the wire and drew a
vivid picture of the importance of this chance which had
come my way. Bristol looked me over with a speculative
eye, as if I were a horse on which someone was advising him
to place his money. I tried to look as promising as possible.
If only he would think me worth betting on. Presently he
nodded. He had, he informed us, eight shillings, which he
was prepared to risk on me. My face fell. Even with his
eight shillings added to our resources, the ticket to London
was a long way off. Madge explained this to him.

"That's all right," said Bristol complacently. "I've a
couple of mates who might be willing to take a flier."

We arranged to meet him and his friends at the railway station within an hour. Madge and I were standing by the ticket office when five British Tommies, with Bristol in the lead, bore down on us.

"There she is," said he, pointing at me. The other five looked me over. Five heads nodded approbation.

Out of the uniform pockets came half crowns and shillings which the Tommies handed over to Madge, my self-constituted financial manager. She counted the money. "Hurray! Enough for a ticket, and fifteen shillings over to see you through your first week in London," she said triumphantly.

While she bought my ticket, I turned to Bristol and his five mates. "Thank you, boys. You'll get your money back. And you won't be sorry you've done this for me. I promise."

"Oh, that's all right," one of the Tommies replied gallantly. "It's always a pleasure to help a lady."

"I mean it," I said earnestly. "I won't forget what you've done for me today. Not ever! And when I'm playing at His Majesty's Theatre in the Haymarket, it'll be because you boys helped me get there."

The six Tommies saw me off on the London Express. I hung out of the window and waved to them, and they all waved back to me.

"Best of luck, Gertie! Mind now, don't let us down."

6

THE LITTLE REVUE in which Lee White and Clay Smith found a place for me was one of the first of a long run of such shows staged by André Charlot. The revue in which I made my first appearance bore the innocuous title, *Some*. This was followed in turn by *Cheep, Tabs,* and *Buzz-Buzz.* I did a toe dance and a duet with Clay Smith, and was also in the chorus. Charlot gave me a three-year contract at three pounds ten shillings a week the first year, four pounds ten shillings the second, and six pounds ten shillings the third. I was made.

The pattern of all these wartime revues was simplicity itself. They were staged with a minimum of scenery and a maximum of taste, and they were cast with star names. Charlot's revues caught on immediately with the British public. Each of them had a long run, and when it closed, it was almost immediately succeeded by another, cut to the same successful pattern.

The masculine part of those revue audiences was almost entirely in khaki. The girls with the young lieutenants in the Gunners and Sappers wore gay evening frocks. The men themselves were home on leave from the Western Front, and were desperately in need of getting the sights and sounds of the battle fronts along the Somme out of their systems. They wanted terribly to forget. They dined and danced and went on to the play and then on to supper clubs, where they danced again and drank, cramming their hours of leave with all the gaiety they could seize. It was up to us in *Charlot's Revue* to offer these men gaiety. It was up to us to bring laughs to boys whose youthful faces were set in grim lines and whose eyes never quite lost the wounded look even when their lips smiled. It was up to us to delude them into believing—if only for one split second—that death and destruction and terror and dirt and pain were unreal.

The boys adored Charlot's revues. We would look out into the house and see a boy sitting in the same seat night after night. We would smile at him across the footlights, establishing a comradeship. Then one night, when we looked, there would be another boy in khaki or navy blue sitting in that seat. The other had gone back, where and to what we didn't know and didn't want to guess. Sometimes, after months, suddenly there he would be again, waiting for us to make him laugh. When he turned up like that, we felt better ourselves and thought: "He's all right. He's come through this time." It never occurred to us, nor did it matter at all, that we didn't even know his name.

The London of June 1944 in which I had found myself on arriving from America bore not the slightest resemblance to the London I remembered during the years 1915 to 1918. The audiences one saw at the West End theaters in the summer of 1944 were predominantly in uniform, but there was a noticeable lack of girls in evening dress, and there was a striking absence of the hectic let-us-dance-and-be-merry-for-tomorrow-we-die gaiety, which was the undercurrent of the life I remembered during World War I. The Londoners of 1944 were quieter and more matter of fact, even about their pleasures. They laughed at the jokes and the songs and the comedy skits in the shows, but you felt no desperation in their amusement. You felt that, not for one minute, though they laughed, did they forget the immediacy of war and the menace to all that the British people hold dear. One felt—at least I did—that between 1917 and 1944 the British people had lost their youth and regained their wisdom.

Bea Lillie was one of the stars of *Some*, and I was required to understudy her as well as appear in the chorus. Bea and I quickly became friends and partners in practical jokes which both of us adored to play on others in the cast.

I remember the night in 1917 when America entered the war. Lee and Clay had sat up all the night before writing a song especially for the occasion, and had rehearsed it all day. The time came for Clay to step out onto the stage and announce the new song. This done, the front tabs were drawn, leaving room downstage for Lee to sing in a spotlight. Bea and I and the rest of the company were standing back of the drop curtains to hear the new song. It was a march entitled "America Answers the Call."

As Lee sang, suddenly Bea started to march madly back and forth back of the curtain just behind Lee. I joined her. The cast began to laugh, and the more they laughed the more exaggerated our marching became. Our arms waved until they moved the curtains. Finally Clay came down upon us.

"My God," he whispered fiercely at Bea, "where do you think you are?"

"The Ritz," she replied with her own inimitable gesture of the right hand, and with that distinctive lift of the voice at the end of the line.

There was a rehearsal call the next day. Although Bea and I lived at opposite ends of London, by sheer coincidence we both arrived late. We were both fired.

The star and her understudy went out to lunch together. I knew Charlot would want to take Bea back, but I was worried about myself. I had gone too far, and I had seriously offended Lee and Clay, who had done so much for me.

Bea and I returned humbly to the theater and I sat in the wardrobe mistress's room waiting to be sent for. Bea was forgiven, and I was lectured severely and then—at Lee White's urgent request—given another trial.

Anyone would think I would have learned something by this experience, but apparently I did not. I was soon up to mischief again.

In one of the revues Lee sang a song, "Have You Seen the Ducks Go By?" At the end of the verse a row of obviously artificial ducks appeared on a wall at the back of the stage and moved across it in time to the music. The effect was made by us girls walking behind the wall, with only our duck-like hats showing. That number was a hopeless temptation to me. I couldn't help making my duck frisk about and behave as no properly drilled duck would ever do. Nor could I resist popping my head up over the wall in the wrong place, winking at the audience, and laughing when they laughed at me. Naturally Lee did not like this in the least. But Bea Lillie adored it and would join in with the chorus and pop her head up—minus the duck headdress. Sometimes she wore a man's straw hat and a false mustache.

The audience would howl with laughter, but it upset Lee. Finally Clay stopped speaking to me.

I suppose a psychologist could find a reason for the irrepressible impulse to play pranks which obsessed me for several seasons after I got started on the London stage. They were the kind of pranks that usually only school children think are funny—fake telegrams, keyholes stuffed with soap, coat sleeves sewed up at the cuffs so that the victim found it impossible to make a quick change of costume. If it seems strange that I should have taken such liberties after I had been at pains to get an opportunity in a London production, I can only explain these idiosyncrasies of mine on the ground that I must have been making up for those years when I had been working at a time when most children my age were playing games. Perhaps it was just something I had to get out of my system. Perhaps, too, it was the not abnormal reaction of a girl who suddenly found herself made much of for the first time in her life. On looking back it seems to me extraordinary the patience which André Charlot had with me during those seasons. I must have been an unmitigated nuisance—to him and to all the other members of the company. What I needed was to have someone tick me off. Ultimately, André Charlot did just that.

During the run of *Some* I kept more or less within bounds. I was still the least important member of the cast. I had every intention of pleasing Mr. Charlot so that he would give me a place in his next revue. I was determined not to go back to touring companies.

I had repaid the loan to Bristol and his mates, who had gone off to Flanders and from whom I received occasional field post cards—the kind supplied to the soldiers—with such messages as: "I am well." "I am ill." "All the best." "Write soon."

It may seem strange that I did not go out to Clapham to find Mother and Dad and let them know that I was now playing in London. What held me back from this was my own ambition. Whenever I was tempted to go back to Mother, Dad, and Granny, it seemed as though something in me would whisper: "Don't go yet. You're not somebody yet. Wait till you're somebody."

I entertained myself imagining the home-coming scene. I would make a royal progress through Clapham in an open taxi. When I arrived at Mother's door there would be a flurry of excitement among the neighbors and Gertrude Lawrence, now the star of the London stage, would descend from her chariot to receive the congratulations of everybody.

Does this seem trivial and selfish? I do not attempt to justify it, or any of the other impulses which made me think such thoughts or do the things I did. Most of us, I believe, have or do still indulge in some such fantasy as this which compensates for a lot of hard knocks and heartaches. Very few among us are noble, or even mature, in all parts of our nature at the same time.

So, though I daydreamed about it, I did not go back to Mother. Mother, however, discovered me. One evening when I arrived at the theater, to make up for the show, a woman was standing just inside the stage door. The doorman whispered she was waiting for me. It was Mother. We stood there in the drafty little passage, with people coming and going and pushing past us, and stared at each other. Suddenly all the years that had passed since the afternoon when I had suddenly conceived the plan of running away and throwing in my lot with my own father were swept away. I was once more a little girl who had done something she knew her mother would not approve of and who had been caught and was now wondering what was going to happen to her.

Actually, nothing happened. To my surprise, Mother took me in her arms. To my question how she had found me, she replied that she had been passing along the street when the air-raid warning sounded. She had taken cover in a hotel next to our theater, and when the all clear came she had stopped out of curiosity to see what was on at the theater. She had noticed the name "Gertie Lawrence" among the small-part people.

My dream of impressing the family was shattered, but at least I had got my mother back, and I realized then how much I had missed her. Granny, grown much older and quite feeble now, took particular personal pride in my having a part in a successful West End production. Though she never said so, I think Granny felt secretly responsible for having started me on my career.

As I went from revue to revue, in each show I was given more to do. This, of course, brought more prestige and, on my part, more self-assurance. I still played pranks, and the more I played, the more daring I became. Not unnaturally, André Charlot got a little fed up with me. He said so more than once in no unvarnished terms.

While I was playing in *Buzz-Buzz*, I came down with a bad attack of lumbago. The doctor ordered me to bed. I was laid up for the better part of a week. When Saturday night came, I was feeling much better than I had felt for several days. The doctor said I would be able to go back to work on Monday. That evening Ivor Novello rang me up. He'd heard I had lumbago, and he wanted to know how I was getting on.

"I'm better," I said. "In fact, I'm working again Monday."

"Wonderful, darling," came Ivor's voice over the wire. "Ethel Baird is opening tonight in her new show, *Summer Time*. Bobbie Andrews and I have got a box. A lot of us are going. Why not come along, too, darling?"

"How can I?" I said.

"But you're much better, darling," Ivor suggested. "My dear girl, do ask the doctor to let you come."

I began to waver. "Of course I *could* ring my doctor and ask him what he thinks," I said.

"Wonderful," Ivor approved. "He's sure to say it would do you no end of good to get out of that stuffy room and have a bit of fun."

"I'll call him," I promised, "and ask him if he thinks it would hurt me to go."

The doctor gave, as his opinion, that I would be no worse if I went to the opening, provided I came straight home and went directly to bed. "No staying out dancing all night," he commanded.

"Oh, I wouldn't think of it," I said hastily.

I promptly rang Ivor and told him to come around and fetch me.

The opening was a very smart one; everybody was there. It was wonderful sitting in the stage box with Ivor, watching the celebrities come in. I was sitting in the front of the box, not to miss a thing, when who should come down the center aisle but Mr. and Mrs. André Charlot. Before I could slither between Ivor and Bobbie into obscurity behind them, André Charlot's eyes were lifted and swept the stage boxes. I felt his gaze halt and fix itself directly on my face. "That's done it," I thought. "He'll be furious, of course."

When Monday evening came, I arrived at the stage door, as chipper as you please. Old George, the doorman, looked at me reprovingly. He blocked the doorway. "I'm sorry, miss," he said. "I've got my orders not to let you in."

"Oh, come off it, George," I said.

Old George shook his head. "Sorry, miss, I've had my orders. Straight from Mr. Charlot himself they came. You're not to be let in. Not any more. You're fired."

"What about my part?" I demanded.

"The understudy is going on for you, miss. She's making up now. Here, I've got a note for you." He produced a sealed envelope and handed it to me.

The note was from André Charlot himself. He made no bones about it. He was firing me from *Buzz-Buzz*. I had been absent more than six performances which, under the terms of my contract, permitted him to cancel it and to engage someone else to take my place. "If you are well enough to go to other people's plays, you are well enough to come to your own," the note ended.

I tried to get him on the telephone, but he was not at his home, and no one there would tell me where he was. Finally, after considerable maneuvering, I located him at a hotel in the country and rang him there. I simply couldn't believe that he would fire me for such a little thing as stay-

ing out one night more than my illness made necessary.
Why, time and again he had forgiven me much worse of-
fenses than that. But now Charlot was offended and angry,
and firm in his determination to teach me a lesson. He gave
me to understand in no uncertain terms that he had had
enough of my nonsense. "You've been asking for this for a
long time," he snapped. Then he hung up, leaving me
gasping.

There was no getting round it. I had been sacked. Already the story was probably traveling like wildfire through
the theaters of the West End. I could just imagine how some
of the wiser ones would smile over the news that Gertrude
Lawrence had been told off for being too smart. "Played
one trick too many, Gertie has."

It was barely a fortnight to Christmas, and I was out of a
job.

7

FROM CAMP TANNER on the estate of the Earl of Chichester our orders were to proceed to Arundel, where a large R.A.F. center was located. On the short drive we passed close to Bognor, with its memories of my childhood holiday when I sang on the sands. Those sands were now barricaded with barbed wire and the sea front was patrolled by guards and protected by big guns.

That night our unit played for the group at Arundel. After the show we visited the "Flare Path" and watched the Spitzes and Mosquitoes coming in from their raids over France. These boys had actually played a part in the great invasion. They had covered the armies swarming up the beaches and fighting their way into the coast towns. And here they were back again. . . .

Two of the boys we talked to in the crew room, where the pilots await their calls for briefing, had bagged Nazi planes that day. They were quiet, modest young men, with bright, clear eyes and ready smiles. Nothing nervy or high-strung about them that anyone could see.

Next day we motored along the south coast, one hundred miles to Canterbury. All Sussex and Kent were a vast armed camp—a sealed reservoir of men and munitions waiting to be ferried over to Normandy. In most of the old churches in the villages we drove through were tombs of Norman knights who had crossed the Channel with William the Conqueror's invaders.

Canterbury was a shock. The town was badly bombed during the last blitz, when Hitler seemed to have decided to go after all England's cathedrals. But here again, as with St. Paul's, he missed. The beautiful minster still stood, proud and lovely in the midst of the surrounding devastation. We did our show under canvas at Bridge Camp. It was all very primitive, but the boys gave us a great hand and were touchingly appreciative of our efforts to entertain them. These men were Commandos and Rangers, boys from every state in the Union, who yowled with delight when I sang them songs they recognized as American. They, too, were awaiting orders to leave for Normandy at any hour.

From Canterbury back to London and a letdown from the high excitement that prevailed all along the south coast. The excitement and singing in the barn near Chichester had given me a sore throat. I gargled sedulously, determined not to be laid up.

This time we headed north into Bedfordshire. The fat farms smiled at us. British people have always loved the countryside, but now you felt that that love was less romantic than formerly. You saw people actually smacking their lips at the sight of rows of broad beans, or six ducklings waddling in single file down a green bank to a pond.

We did our show in Bedford's city hall that night to an audience of twenty-six hundred mixed troops. The mayor and mayoress were there and there were speeches and photographs and flowers—really a gala.

I got back late to The Swan, not feeling at all well. Fortunately we had a quiet night—no air raids. We were all up early the next morning to motor twenty-three miles back to Luton to put on a factory show at "Electrolux." Luton, with its wonderful views of the Chilterns, used to manufacture hats, both felt and straw. The straw was imported from Japan and from Italy—one reason why the Luton workers are not turning out straw boaters this season. Luton still makes its own beer, and very good beer it is, especially after you've been singing out of doors to a lunch-hour crowd.

We put on another show that night for the R.A.F. in a non-operational base. The temperature in the hut was 102 degrees. I went home after the show and to bed, where I stayed for the next four days. I kept begging Mary Barrett to dose me and to cover up the fact that I was ill. I went through anxious hours, hoping the press wouldn't get hold of the story. If that had happened, it might have prevented me from getting to the second front, as I had been promised.

From Bedford we drove more than two hundred miles back to the busy south coast and the Southampton area. We found everyone there talking about the new "pilotless planes" which were beginning to come over and about which there had been rumors. There were three alerts during our first night in Portsmouth. The south coast had always been a target for the Luftwaffe, but the boys along that coast were watching for the "doodlebugs," as the Americans called them. The things were proving more deadly than had been expected. As they exploded on contact, or on time, and without warning, it was almost impossible to find safety if one were caught within distance of the

blast. There were a lot of casualties in and around Southampton and, we heard, in London. Our Red Cross nurse at
Drury Lane was killed by one of them.

For a week we did shows in tents, hangars, garrison theaters, and under trees. Each time the men would be gone the
next morning. It gave one a sinking feeling to realize that
these men were actually going into battle with the song in
their hearts they had heard you sing only a few hours before. I had brought a new song with me when I came back
to the big Southampton area, "All's Well, Mademoiselle." It
was written for me on D-Day by Michael Carr and Tommy
Connor. I had thousands of copies printed, and as I sang it I
handed out the autographed copies to the boys and got them
to sing it with me:

> *All's well, mademoiselle,**
> *We're on our way to dear old gay Paree.*
> *All's well, mademoiselle,*
> *We've started off for Normandy.*
> *It won't be long till victory.*
> *Hearts will sing that happy day,*
> *France will ring with the "Marseillaise."*
> *All's well, mademoiselle.*
> *Soon you will dance again,*
> *Love and romance again,*
> *Vive la France again,*
> *Mademoiselle.*

My diary gives the story of my experience in London
when the robots began to rain down on the city:

*Reprinted by permission of the copyright owners, Peter Maurice
Music Co., Ltd., and Peter Maurice, Inc.

. . . Sunday night. I am in bed at the Savoy. 10:00 P.M. Alert just gone. Wonder if it's Hitler's dirty flying bugs again? The window in my bedroom is broken from the blast concussion. But part of Cherbourg is ours tonight; so who cares? . . . 1:00 A.M. Three of the bloody things have just fallen outside. You hear the beastly droning; then it stops; then it explodes. The whole hotel shudders and my curtains blow into the room from the blast. . . . 1:50 A.M. One more has just blazed over and dropped with a terrific bang near by. The Strand seems to be the popular target for tonight! Next door a couple are making love. *Here comes another!* And now it's raining hard to make things harder for the A.R.P. rescue workers. That couple must be fatalists. Wouldn't Hitler be furious at their complete unconcern? . . . There's another. That makes six around here up to now. And our Combined Air Forces are supposed to have been hammering at the robot bases every day. . . . *Seven!* More rain. Quiet next door now. *Eight!* What a night! Haven't heard a shot from our guns, but I don't see how they can spot them. The projectiles just seem to come over like fireworks on the fifth of November. *Nine!* It is now two-fifteen. Not much lull. The krauts must be having a gleeful evening across the Channel. This kind of warfare costs them no pilots. I wonder if Hitler has it all arranged so that he can sit at home and push a button that fires the wretched things? *Ten* and *eleven.* Two at once that time. Now they are coming in pairs. It's no use trying to sleep in a tin hat, and it looks pretty silly, especially when one is alone, so I shall just have to sit up and record this my first real experience of being blindly blitzed by robots. . . .

It really is a strange and utterly helpless feeling—not one sound of a plane of ours overhead, or any attempt at gunfire; just these oncoming, droning, phantom missiles loaded with destruction. My room is on a small courtyard, so I can see nothing, but the explosions have been very violent. Much damage must be being done. Being Sunday, and this a business section, there may not be many casualties, but the property loss will be great. It is now 2:45 A.M. It gets light around 5:00 A.M. Soon I can open my curtains and get some fresh air. Not that the daylight stops the "doodlebugs."

I was just going to write "guess it's all over for tonight," but here comes Charlie again, making a round dozen since one o'clock. The alert has been on since ten—five hours steady. I'm getting very sleepy. . . . Here's another one coming—thirteen. I admit I got out of and under the bed that time. It was too close to be comfortable, and I don't like odd numbers. But it passed right overhead and *crumped* down farther away. Golly! That seemed like "this is it" for a while.

3:45 A.M. Maybe I should put down the date—Monday, June 26. *Sixteen* and *seventeen* sound as if they had landed right outside. I can hear the A.R.P. at work. Those last two were volcanic. How many more? I suppose this is reprisal for Cherbourg.

Four o'clock just chimed, and number *eighteen* has come down with an awful bump. It must have hit a power station or something. This is truly a nightmare. The air is full of sudden death, coming at us from all sides, without cessation. I hope I have the nerve to take this kind of bombing, especially when I'm alone. I get to thinking . . . thinking . . .

Lying awake in the ghostly half-light alone, listening for the drone of the buzz bombs as they came over, holding myself tense through the moment of agonizing suspense, waiting for the crash of their landing, I found myself living through the air raid that rocked London the night my daughter Pamela was born.

WHEN André Charlot canceled my contract with him, I immediately went over to the London Hippodrome to see if I could get a part in the Christmas production, which was due to open there in a few days. But I was told there was nothing for me. A few more inquiries made it clear to me that it wasn't going to be easy to land a job immediately. The news had gone round that I was impossible to manage.

I needed to get to work right away. I had very little money saved up, barely enough to keep me if I remained out of work for more than a fortnight. I have never been thrifty. Goodness knows I wish I were. From the day I began to work and to earn money, I've always spent what I earned. I don't think it ever occurred to me that I would be out of work and unable to earn a living. So, as the money came in, it went out—for myself and for others, and for things that seemed to me necessary, or interesting, or worth while.

Though there were no openings at the theaters, I thought I might have some success as an entertainer at Murray's Club. Murray's was London's first night club. It had just been started, and it was drawing big crowds, especially the young officers on leave. I went round to see the manager and was auditioned. He engaged me to start at once. He was glad to get a youngster from *Charlot's Revue* who might be expected to draw trade. There I directed and put on the first floor show in a London night club.

At the same time I understudied Phyllis Dare in the Hippodrome pantomime.

Murray's was a gay spot in wartime London. It was the smart place to go for supper and dancing, a place where the music and the girls and the wine and the cabaret helped people forget the heartbreaking defeat at Kut-el-Amara and the blow to British prestige.

It was one of the tensest periods of the war. Everyone felt it. Everyone was edgy, nervous, overtired, and desperately determined to keep up a front at any cost, so the theater flourished. One night André Charlot appeared at Murray's and asked me to join him at his table. He said he wanted to make up, and I was as glad about this as he obviously was. I wanted us to be friends, and I wanted—and said so frankly— to get a place in his next revue. But, alas, there was nothing for me in it. I've often wondered if Charlot wasn't just being canny; whether he wasn't determined to find out, before he re-engaged me, whether I really had settled down and could be trusted to behave myself.

Meanwhile, I got together a double act with Walter Williams, who had been in some of Charlot's revues. We opened at the London Coliseum and toured the circuit of the Moss Empire theaters which were scattered through the key cities. The act was an enormous success. We used numbers from old Charlot's revues, and as we were billed "straight from London," we always topped every bill. I danced, and Walter's big hit song was "K-K-Katie."

(Poor Walter was killed by a direct-bomb hit during the London blitz three years ago. When he went I lost a great friend who helped me when I needed it.)

At that time my own personal life was occupying more and more of my attention. I was engaged to a boy who was serving in the balloon barrage which floated over London. Whenever I would look up and see the big balloons bobbing lazily above the roofs and spires, like bubbles rising in an enormous glass of champagne, I had a cozy feeling of protection. My boy was up there looking out for me and for our city. He had taken me to meet his parents; he'd given me a ring—a sapphire surrounded by little diamonds—which I adored and wore proudly. Someday, when the war was over, we'd get married. Meanwhile, we were together whenever his hours permitted it. He'd turn up at Murray's, or I'd come off the stage at one of the London music halls where Walter Williams and I were playing, and there would be Peter sitting in the dressing room, waiting for me.

Then all at once something happened—I met Frank Howley. He was twenty years my senior and I was immensely flattered by his attention. Moreover, he belonged to my world—the world of the theater. He spoke my language—that of the theater. He was a director, and he talked to me of his future plans in which I figured as his star.

When I went out with Peter, he was not interested in hearing me talk about the theater. He didn't take the theater seriously, and he couldn't understand why I did. His plan for us was to get married and for me to leave the profession at once in order to turn myself into the conventional type of young wife—the kind of wife his people would approve of for him. The more I thought of it, the surer I became that this was no part that I would ever star in.

Frank had no family problem. His brothers approved of me, though they exclaimed with surprise on meeting me: "My God, Frank, she doesn't wear any make-up!"

The more I thought about Peter and the life he pictured to me, and to which he, apparently, looked forward as though it was the most wonderful existence in the world, the more certain I became that it was not the life for me. So I broke our engagement. Peter took it hard, but gallantly. He was a romantic, and he refused to let me give him back his ring. "Keep it," he said, "and wear it to remember me by. I shall remember you always."

Frank and I were married—quietly and without interrupting my work. Mother disapproved, but there was nothing she could do about it, as I was economically independent. She thought Frank was too old for me, and she reminded me of her own unfortunate marriage with my father, who was also in the profession.

There's no doubt Mother would have liked me to have been young Mrs. Peter. It would have justified all her efforts to bring me up like a lady. Granny, however, had had her misgivings about my engagement to Peter from the start. Granny liked people who knew what world they belonged to, and who stayed inside that world. "You may not be wealthy with Frank," she said to me quietly, "but money isn't everything. It isn't the most important thing in life. Not nearly so important as doing what you feel you have to do as well as you're able to do it."

We went to live in Maida Vale. We had a flat, and Frank's two brothers stayed with us whenever they were in London. Frank began looking around for financial backing to start a company of his own. Meanwhile, I went on with my theater work, doing my job as a housewife, and understudying Bea Lillie, whom Charlot was featuring in the current show. I was terribly grateful to Charlot for taking me on again, and I kept hoping he would find a real place for me in one of the revues before long. I didn't wish Bea any bad luck, but I couldn't help longing for a chance to show Charlot—and the audience—what I could do. In that ambition, and in the fantasies that I built up around it, I suppose I was just like every other understudy in the world.

Then I learned I was going to have a child. I was excited and thrilled.

"You should give up your work," the doctor advised.

"How can I?" I shrugged my shoulders. I couldn't explain that my husband was not earning anything at the time.

The doctor frowned. "It is usually possible to do whatever it is necessary to do," he said. "At least I have found this to be true."

"Oh, I agree with you," I told him.

If my own experience had taught me anything, it was that, if a thing had to be done, it could be done. Of course it would be wonderful to be so well off you could coddle yourself. But then I had never been in that state of financial ease. Doctors, I told myself, were always telling you to rest and relax and not to worry. They gave you that sort of advice spontaneously and freely. It was part of the formula. They must know that a young, struggling actress couldn't possibly stop working for months simply because she was going to have a baby. I had known dozens of girls who had gone on working until just before their babies were born. I compromised by promising myself that I would work as long as I could; then I would stay home and obey the doctor's orders.

Meantime, I had a great deal to keep me occupied. The flat took a lot of attention. We couldn't afford a servant, not even a daily. I did all the cooking, and, in addition, I made my baby's clothes—sewing them by hand with all the dainty stitches Granny had taken such pains to teach me. There was no money to waste, but I wanted my baby to have the best I could give it. I bought a wicker clothes-basket and lined it with padding and covered it with pink silk to make a bassinet, like the expensive ones I had seen in the shops in Regent Street.

One evening, when it came time to start for the theater, I felt very ill. I said to myself, "I can't possibly go to work tonight." As general understudy I was under contract to report at the theater for every performance in case I was needed.

Then I thought, "I'll have to call up the theater. That means I've got to go out to the corner to the telephone. By the time I've dressed and done that, I might as well hop a bus and go there, report, and come home again."

It was late when I arrived, which was unusual for me. I should have checked in at seven-thirty, but it was ten minutes of eight when I turned into the alley which led to the stage door. There was the stage manager, walking up and down, muttering and fuming. There was the callboy, running this way and that. Several heads stuck out of dressing-room windows. Then the stage manager caught sight of me.

"For God's sake!" he yelled. "Come on! Where the hell have you been?"

I started to tell him I was ill, but he paid no attention. Instead, he caught hold of my elbow, hurried me up the steps and in through the stage door.

"Lillie's off," he shouted. "Went riding in Hyde Park, and the horse threw her. Concussion, they say she's got. You've got to go on. We're holding the curtain for you. Buck up, my girl. Here's your chance. Remember we're counting on you."

My chance—the chance I'd longed for for years. The chance every understudy dreams about—the star suddenly ill, or meeting with an accident, and the little understudy having to step in and take her place. Now this had happened to me. As I stood there in Bea's dressing room and her dresser helped me with swift, experienced fingers, I thought, "The irony of it. It has happened to me just now when I am feeling so ill." The dresser looked at me encouragingly.

"You'll be all right, miss."

In a couple of songs Bea was doing male impersonations. For these she wore a white tie and tails. The black broadcloth suit was cut perfectly and fitted her slim, straight body like a glove. I held my breath while the dresser laced me up tightly; then I got into the trousers and white waistcoat. I stood before the long mirror and looked at myself critically. Yes, I would do.

When my call came, I went on, and for the first time in my life on the stage I knew anxiety. Bea was a tremendous favorite. Most of the audience had come on purpose to see her. Could I satisfy them? If I could hold that audience, if I could make them laugh and applaud and like Gertrude Lawrence, then the rest of my career was assured. If I failed, well—— My cue came and I went on.

Standing in the wings, watching with a worried look on his face, was André Charlot. I flashed him a smile. At eleven-thirty, after the final curtain, André Charlot kissed me on both cheeks and said: "Well done, Gertie."

That night, and for many nights thereafter, I sang and danced and tossed my lines across the footlights with all the gaiety at my command. I was no longer anxious—that first night had proved to me that I could hold the audience. I could make them laugh, applaud, and cheer, and come back for more. I was doing it. I had succeeded. The worried look was gone from Charlot's face.

The fall from her horse had injured Bea Lillie so badly that she had to be out of the show for several months. This meant that Charlot would have to engage another star to replace her—a big name—unless I, the understudy, could take the place and hold the public. If I could, then my reputation and prestige were made.

Night after night I bit my lips while the dresser laced me so tightly it was hard to get breath enough to sing. Each night, when I came off the stage, Frank would be there, waiting. There came a night when I was very ill and Frank round a taxi for us. I sank into the corner of the seat and folded my arms around myself tightly, trying to stop the pain. Frank was arguing with the driver, who, as usual in wartime, objected to going so far. He offered him five shillings extra, and grudgingly the man agreed to take us. Frank got in beside me and put his arms around my waist. His tenderness was a comfort, and the warm pressure of his hands eased the pain. Suddenly the electric light in the back of the cab was switched on; the driver drew up and swung around in his seat. "Now then, none of that, you two," he growled. "Not in my cab you don't."

"What's the matter?" Frank demanded.

"Never mind what's the matter," said the driver. "You know all right. I seen ya in the mirror, I did."

"Listen," said Frank, his voice steely. "This lady happens to be my wife."

"Coo," said the driver. "Lady, my word! I've heard that tale before. Get on with you now, get out of my cab."

"We're not getting out. You've agreed to take us to Maida Vale, and that is what you are going to do. I've told you, this lady is my wife. She's going to have a baby, and I've got to get her home as fast as you can make it."

The driver shot a questioning look at me. I nodded. "If you don't get me there soon," I said, "I'm afraid I shall faint."

The driver switched off the light, stepped on the accelerator, and the cab shot out of the Edgeware Road with a jolt that nearly landed me on the floor. I gasped out loud. "My God, Missus, don't have it in my cab," the cabby yelled.

The air raids on London were increasing. There was a battery of anti-aircraft guns in the court outside our windows. The noise they made prevented anyone from sleeping, and there was always the danger of shrapnel from our own shells as well as from the German bombs. I began to get jumpy, especially after a piece of shrapnel came sailing into our room one night and embedded itself in the wall.

One day Frank told me he had got word of something in Liverpool that might be good. At least, it sounded promising. He went off to look it over. His two brothers were staying with us in Maida Vale, but both of them were down with influenza. I went to the theater that night as usual. I did not feel at all well, but some of that I laid to the fact that I had had a lot to do in the house that day, getting Frank off and nursing his two brothers. My urge was to clean everything. I took down the curtains from the windows, washed them, and hung them up again, wet. I went over all the things I had prepared for the baby. For several nights past I had not slept well, as the Zeps had been coming over. I felt so faint while I was dressing, the dresser became alarmed. She brought me out a stiff drink of brandy, and insisted that I take it just before going on. The brandy warmed me and keyed up my spirits. I gave one of my best performances. I knew it was my last night because Bea was returning the following Monday. The house kept applauding and calling me back for an encore. Twice—three times I went back. I could see the stage manager standing in the wings, smiling broadly. When I got back to the dressing room to change, and the excitement began to wear off, I felt very ill indeed.

"It's good it's a Saturday night," the dresser said. "You can go home and rest all day tomorrow and Monday."

"That's true," I said gratefully.

When I left the theater, the street was dark and quiet. I stood there, wishing a taxi would come by, but none came. Every minute I felt worse and worse. The thought of going out to Maida Vale, going in a bus if no taxi was to be found, was more than I could endure. I thought, "I'd better go home to Mother. She'll look after me until Frank gets back from Liverpool." A bus came by, going toward Piccadilly, and I hopped aboard. I would have to change at Piccadilly Circus for Clapham. I got out there and joined the crowd at the curb, praying I wouldn't have to wait long. Minutes passed. Busses for Richmond and Shepherd's Bush and Peckham, busses for the Elephant and Castle, busses for Hounslow and Ealing and Wormwood Scrubs came lumbering down on us, stopped to let off and take on passengers, and went lumbering on again. Every minute I waited increased the agony of physical pain and terror. The bobby kept looking at me anxiously.

"Where do you want to go, miss?" he inquired.

"Clapham." Then I added, "I'm ill. I'm going to have a baby."

"Then you shouldn't go there by bus," said the bobby practically.

"I know," I said, "but the taxis don't want to go so far."

The law blew its whistle. A cruising taxi came obediently to the curb. The bobby opened the door and helped me in. He gave the driver the address, and then out of respect to a lady's feelings he whispered something, confidentially, in the driver's ear.

We started, and the man spoke over his shoulder to me: "I'll get you there, lady. I'm a married man myself."

Mother was home when I got there, and Dad let me in. Mother took one look at me, and not waiting for me to say anything, she called Dad to make haste and hold the taxi. "You'll go right to the nursing home," she said to me, "tonight."

"But," I objected, "the baby isn't due for nearly two months."

"Nonsense," said Mother; "you can't tell a thing about a first baby." She bustled me out and into the taxi again and on to a nursing home, where I was immediately put to bed.

That night, and through the next, the Germans treated London to one of the worst air raids of the war. On Monday night, while the raid was at its height, my daughter was born. The sound she heard on coming into this world was the crash of bombs. All her life she has loathed the sound of planes.

No one, apparently, had thought to notify André Charlot that I was in a nursing home. On Sunday and Monday I had been much too ill to think of anything. On Tuesday morning I received a card from the stage manager to remind Miss Lawrence that a rehearsal had been called for Monday, at which she had failed to appear. The doctor sent a letter in reply, saying that Miss Lawrence had been otherwise engaged on Monday!

On Tuesday Frank came to see me, bringing a bunch of poppies. Of course he was pleased about the baby, but he was terribly worried too. He sat by my bed, looking very downcast. The prospect in Liverpool had turned out to be another disappointment.

"How long will you have to stay here?" he asked.

"Ten days," I told him. The doctor had said, "Three weeks," but I knew I must get back to work before that.

Frank's face grew longer. He hadn't a bean, and we were behind with the rent. His brothers were still laid up, and they had no money either. "I don't know which way to turn," he said.

I was unable to suggest anything. All I wanted was to be allowed to stay there in that cool, clean bed—and rest. I was so tired. My hands, lying on the coverlet, seemed too heavy to lift. On the left hand, next to my wedding ring, was the sapphire ring Peter had given me. Silently I drew it off and held it out to my husband. There was no need to say anything. Frank dropped the sapphire into his waistcoat pocket and the anxiety lifted from his face. He bent, kissed my cheek, and went away.

I never saw Peter's ring again.

9

WE NAMED THE BABY PAMELA. It was a beautiful, romantic name. She was to have two others—Barbara after her father's sister who was a nun, and May because she had arrived in that proverbially merry month.

Just then the name Pamela did not seem at all suitable for the tiny bluish little scrap of humanity which I held to my breast so proudly.

Premature babies, I was informed, were difficult to rear. They had to have special care, special food, and constant surveillance. Dr. Ambrose said bluntly that the reason Pamela was a seven-months baby was because I had worked so hard, coupled with the strain of the air raids.

During the fortnight I was in the nursing home I had time to take stock of a great many things. First, my responsibility toward my child. Pam required expert, expensive care, and this meant I would have to get back to work as soon as possible. I had brought her into the world; she belonged to me as no one and nothing else in my life ever had belonged. I would fight to keep her alive and to help her grow up strong and beautiful.

André and Madame Charlot were real friends. Though they never mentioned it, they were aware of my predicament. Charlot let me go back to work as understudy, and I had reason to believe he meant to give me a real part of my own in the new show. I was still pretty weak, naturally, but overjoyed at the slim silhouette the mirror now presented.

To meet the new expenses connected with Pamela, the flat in Maida Vale would have to be given up. We could live with Mother and Dad for a time and the baby could stay in the nursing home. This, I thought, would set Frank's mind at rest, and he would be free to take on the direction of companies on tour.

By the time I was ready to leave the nursing home I had it all worked out, but Frank objected. Therefore I left the nursing home with Pamela, returned to the flat, and tried for several weeks to carry on. I did my housework, bathed, fed, and walked the baby until midday. Then Mother would come over and take care of the baby while I went to work. After a while it became obvious we couldn't continue in this way, so we gave up the flat and went to live with Mother and Dad. Her dining room on the ground floor was turned into a bedroom for us. After a few more weeks we decided to put the baby back in the nursing home, where she would get expert care.

On my free days I would go to the nursing home to visit Pamela. The matron didn't encourage visitors. The home was understaffed, owing to the war, and the nurses were overworked. That was the year of the influenza epidemic, and visitors in hospitals and nursing homes, who might carry the infection to patients, were not encouraged. Either Mother or I called around at the nursing home to inquire about the baby every few days. Between those times we satisfied our curiosity by means of telephone calls.

Frank had not been successful in finding something he wanted to do. Finally the break came.

"It's no good going on like this," he said. "We're not getting anywhere."

I could see he was hurt, but I had all I could do just then to take care of myself and to pay the bills for Pamela at the nursing home. Frank finally left. He said we wouldn't hear from him again in a hurry. A few days later I caught the flu and didn't dare visit my baby.

It was several days later that Mother went round in my behalf to the nursing home to pay the bill and to inquire about Pam's progress.

"The baby's not here," the matron said.

"Not here?" Mother was incredulous.

"Certainly not. You didn't expect to find her here, did you?"

"What's become of her?" Mother demanded.

"The child's father came the day before yesterday and took her away."

Mother hurried back to the house to tell me what the matron had said.

"It can't be true!" I objected. "I'm paying for the baby's care. How could Frank—or anyone—take her away?"

I got up out of bed and Mother and I went to see the matron. "Where did he take the baby?" I demanded.

She told me briskly: "To Liverpool. I understand the child's father's parents live there."

Somehow I felt Frank wouldn't do a thing like that. The matron was very short with me—suspiciously so. When I demanded more definite information, she finally confessed that the baby was still in the home, but she was under strict orders from the child's father not to allow me to see her.

When there was nothing to be done with the matron, I

went to the police station. There I was told that, under the law, a father could exercise complete jurisdiction over his child. The fact that I had paid the bills at the nursing home did not alter the law. However, the court granted me permission to see my child. Mother and I returned to the nursing home and brandished the court order in the face of the matron and I demanded my rights. She was a tall, bony, equine woman, and she obviously found us a great nuisance. She said stonily: "That baby is no longer here."

"You told me that before," I reminded her. "Later, you said the child was here. Surely you don't expect me to believe you now."

"No," she said justly. "I can quite see why you wouldn't, but you can come with me and see for yourself."

We went through the nursery but there was no sign of Pamela. The matron had obviously telephoned Frank and he had told her to hide the child from me.

I went back to the police station. Surely, I said, something could be done to help me find my child, but again I was brought face to face with the British law—because Frank was Pamela's father, he was legally allowed to dispose of her as he wished without consulting me.

I went posthaste to the lodgings where I thought Frank had been living since we broke up. He was no longer there. Both his brothers were away on tour. I wrote Frank in care of his mother, the only address I knew where he might be reached. There was no answer to my letter.

Weeks passed. No word from Frank. I went through my routine at the theater night after night like a robot.

Each day I told myself that there would surely be a message from Frank before that night. But none came. Every evening when I went to the theater I fortified myself with the thought that when I came off the stage at the end of the performance I would find Frank waiting for me in my dressing room as he used to wait in the old days.

Then one afternoon when I came off stage old George was waiting for me with a telegram. I read it in a glance:

CHILD DESPERATELY ILL NEEDS YOU MEET ME USUAL PLACE FRANK.

I knew he meant Lyons' Corner House in Piccadilly, where he and I used to meet and in which we had planned our wedding.

I tossed out the contents of my purse and counted the money. It amounted to very little. I knew the pawnshop which was situated conveniently close to the stage door would still be open. We girls often took our trinkets there and thus raised a little much-needed cash.

I laid a chain purse and my watch on the counter and asked the man what he would let me have on them. There was no need for him to inspect the pieces; he knew them well. They had been in and out of his vault times without number. He automatically counted out thirty shillings.

It was all he usually allowed on the things, but in this case it was not enough for my purposes. If Pamela were desperately ill, as the wire stated, she would need doctors, a nurse, special medicines. All those things spelled money. I would need more than thirty shillings.

"Can't you give me more on them just this once?" I pleaded.

He shook his head at me. "You know better than that, young lady."

"But I need the money desperately. Thirty shillings isn't enough. I've got to have a fiver at least. Come on, be a sport."

Without a word he slid the things back across the counter.

"You mean you won't?"

"Not me," he said. Then, unable to resist the impulse to scold those who have committed the sin of being in need of money, he said severely, "I've got ter teach you girls a lesson, I 'ave. The management pays you, don't it? Of course it do. What does a girl like you do with her money? Throws it around. You ought to be ashamed of yourself, you ought. You'd ought to have a tidy little sum put by in the savings bank, and not come round expecting me to give you fancy prices on stuff that's not worth the half of it."

He was working himself up into a fine state of righteous indignation. Meanwhile time was passing. And I had to have the money.

I laid my little bits of jewelry back on the counter and put my problem to him unashamedly.

"I'll tell you what I do with my money," I said. "I have a baby. She's only a few months old. She's ill. Desperately ill. If you don't believe me, here's the wire from my husband to prove it."

I pulled the crumpled telegram out of my pocket and held it out to him. "Go on, read it."

Deliberately he adjusted his spectacles and read Frank's message.

"I've got to go to her, don't you see. I've got to have the money. That's why I've come to you."

Without a word he turned and unlocked his money drawer. He took out five dirty pound notes and put them in my hand. Then he gathered up the jewelry and handed it over.

I started to thank him, but he cut me off.

"Take this stuff along with you. You can pay me back later." He disappeared into the darkness of the already closing shop.

It was a white-faced, thoroughly frightened Frank who rose from the table to meet me when I arrived at the teashop. Neither of us spoke for a while. There was too much to say. Finally I asked, "Where's my baby, Frank? Where is she?"

He replied, "She's still in the nursing home. She's been there all the time."

I stared at him, unable to believe my ears. He then confessed that he had hoped, by taking the child, to bring me back to him. Now he had found out that he could not keep up the payments in the nursing home. Also the baby was ailing and he had promised the matron to send for me.

Once again, and for the last time, he put it up to me:

"If you can lend me some money, I can go away and open an academy in the Midlands," he said. "And I won't trouble you and Pamela any more."

I gave him all I had—the contents of my purse. And there our life together ended in the same spot where we had planned our marriage.

10

TRULY, a marvelous play could be written after the pattern of *Grand Hotel*, about the characters one finds in the hostels on the south coast of England during these days of war. Members of all the services come in at all times and in all sorts of dress. Many of them are straight from the invasion front. Tired, dirty, hungry, thirsty, the men line up at the desk, asking for beds and baths. The invariable reply is: "Sorry. No rooms."

But though there are no rooms, and never a sufficient number of beds for the war weary, by some sort of juggling process that borders on the miraculous places are made for the newcomers. War has turned the old Box and Cox situation, which was the basis of so many farces, into an everyday reality. One man drags himself, yawning, out of bed to make place for another whose only claim is that he is, if possible, even wearier than the earlier comer.

The bar opens at twelve noon. By one-thirty the stock on the shelves is completely sold out. And still the men keep coming, pathetically hopeful of rest and refreshment. The hotel lobby is strewn with duffel bags and other gear, which everyone stumbles over. The swing doors revolve ceaselessly.

At all hours of the day and night a queue waits with

varying degrees of patience before the door marked *Bath*. Standing in line, waiting my turn at the tub, I thought: It's like the Cats' Home. We girls used to queue up like this before the one bath to a floor. How often I've stood on the cold, linoleum-covered passage, warming one foot against the other, and sighed: "Shall I ever be rich enough to have a bath of my own?"

It was good to get back to work after being laid up with a froggy throat, and thrilling to be back in the south coast area, which was now part of the second front. One morning I was told that arrangements had been made for us to go out to H.M.S. *Thyne*. The admiral's barge was sent to fetch us and we gave our first show at sea. Three hundred and fifty jolly jack-tars and their officers crammed the little theater-chapel-lecture cabin.

Motoring back to London, one saw evidences on all sides of the destruction wrought by the robot planes. The crowded districts of London were again hard hit. We passed squares in which all the little houses and shops were ruined. Though the bombs had fallen hours earlier, they were still carrying the dead from the ruins. But what broke my heart were the little homes, roofless, and exposed to the elements. It had been raining for forty-eight hours. Somehow there was something cruelly indecent about the exposure of those rooms with their pathetic furnishings. You knew that each of these wrecked homes had cost its owner all his life and his savings to acquire.

In the bombed-out districts neighbors were helping each other, sharing the misfortune, the anxiety, and the tragedy of death. The robots had broken the reserve which has always been a characteristic of British life. "Keep yourself to yourself," Mother used to say.

It is one more evidence of the enormity of the disaster which London has undergone in this war that these people of Clapham and Wandsworth and Tooting no longer keep themselves to themselves. Everyone's misfortune now is shared by everyone.

Though the rain poured pitilessly, children dug in the rubble seeking clothing and toys. One man, after working for hours, had just found his dog buried under a heap of timbers. The poor creature was terribly injured. The man mercifully wrung its neck while he cursed the Nazis.

I put in another sleepless night at the Savoy. The alert sounded at 1:00 A.M., and the bombs came over with clock-like precision every few minutes, until noon. Bush House was hit, and other buildings in the Strand. Still the rain continued.

It was still pouring when our unit left London at two in the afternoon, headed for Leeds and then for Catterick Camp, the great military center in Yorkshire.

When I woke next morning in the Queen's Hotel in Leeds, the sun was shining. I felt happy as a lizard when he comes out of a clammy crack in a wall and feels the sun's warmth on his body.

Mary Barrett tapped on my door and called: "Happy birthday!" I had quite forgotten.

It was July Fourth, my birthday, the birthday of the American nation. It was also the anniversary of my marriage to Richard. All day I looked and hoped for some message from him. There were cables from my daughter Pamela and from many friends in America. Also a letter from Jack Potter, manager of *Lady in the Dark*. But none from Richard. I knew what that meant—he was at sea. But I also knew, wherever he was, and whatever his duties, he was remembering the day and keeping it in his heart. As I was.

Poor Richard, I thought. He hasn't had much of a marriage with me up to now. We had only a short time together before Pearl Harbor. Since that day the war has occupied him. We have been like thousands of other couples, living on letters, building all our plans on the words: "after the war."

Mary gave me my first birthday present that day—a silver five-shilling piece, very rare. The news leaked out that it was my birthday, and some of the men serenaded me and gave me flowers. There was one red, white, and blue bouquet which reminded me of the floral American flag which Archie Selwyn sent me on the Fourth of July before I made my first trip to America.

At Catterick I ran into Major Peter Mather, who was Helen Hayes's touring manager in *Victoria Regina*. He was eager to talk and ask about America and his friends there— Gilbert and Kitty Miller, Ruth Gordon, and a lot more. We discussed the great amount of good Helen had done for England by touring America with *Victoria Regina*. There is no doubt that an honest, well-conceived play, which really represents the psychology of a nation, does more to reveal the spirit of that nation to the people of other countries than all the painfully and artfully built-up propaganda put out by government bureaus. The American audiences who saw *Victoria Regina* were in a better position to understand Britain. It is tragic that no play to date has been written which honestly reveals the American spirit to the British audiences. I hope not one but many plays will be written and produced which, by revealing the American character and what goes on inside American minds and hearts, will make America more understandable to the British people.

Thinking along these lines, after my talk with Peter Mather, it occurred to me suddenly: "I wonder if people thought this way during and just after the last war. Or were we so cocksure the tragedy couldn't happen again that we forgot about the need of understanding between our two nations?"

During that winter which followed the armistice and before the unemployment crisis threatened England, London, as I remember, was full of Americans. Many of these were on leave before going home. Behind them, as behind the British men one met, were the horror, filth, and weariness of war. They wanted, above all, to forget. They wanted to be gay. . . .

11

NOVEMBER 11, 1918. The war was over. Everyone wanted to forget what war was like and the sorrows it had brought. Everyone was determined not to be downhearted, not to worry about the state of the postwar world, or the future. It was true most of the men one met at parties were either definitely middle-aged or obviously too young to have been in the war, and for every man, at every party, there were half-a-dozen girls. No one complained about this—it was one of the things you had to take, one of the things four years of war had done to British life. But this lack of men and the superabundance of women had the effect of making the women vie with one another to attract the attention of the men even more than women had done in other periods. This keen competition made society more brilliant, put an edge on parties. People did things and amused themselves in ways that would have seemed incredible five or six years before. Many of the old social barriers were down and the field was open to all riders.

I reveled in the gaiety, which meant all the more to me because of the strain I had been living under after the baby was born. I had taken a little flat on the fringe of Mayfair. Pam was still with Mother, and Granny was thrilled to have her.

The newspapers and illustrated weeklies were making a great to-do over Princess Mary's forthcoming marriage to Lord Lascelles. It was exactly the kind of event calculated to fill Granny with delight and to interest her for weeks on end. H.R.H., the Prince of Wales, was the leader of the young set in London which had by now opened its doors to me.

P.W., as his intimates referred to him, had fulfilled all the promise I had found in those early photographs of him which I used to pin up beside my mirror. He was debonair, amusing, charming. He and his favorite younger brother, the Duke of Kent, went about in London's night life, enjoying themselves and spreading pleasure wherever they went.

My dressing room at the theater had two entrances—one from the passage leading to the stage; the other, an emergency exit, which opened directly from the alley. Many evenings the Prince of Wales and the Duke of Kent would come up the alley, and old George, the doorman, would let them in. I'll never forget dashing into my dressing room one night between scenes to find the Duke of Kent seated before my mirror, trying on a wig of long, false curls. The other members of his party were bedeviling poor Florrie, my dresser. I had been presented to the Prince of Wales by Captain Philip Astley, whom I had met at Mrs. Walter Guinness', and I can still see the long music room, with its gleaming parquet floor, and Elsa Maxwell at the piano, as I walked across it that night with Beatrice Guinness, who whispered, "Gertrude, I want you to meet the handsomest man in London."

Philip was in the Guards. He **was** everything a knight in

armor should be, as dreamed of by a young romantic girl. He was born at Chequers, which is now the official country home of all British prime ministers. He was christened in the robes of Oliver Cromwell, and educated at Eton and the Royal Military College, added to which he was desperately good-looking, and had unparalleled charm. We had to fall in love with each other. It was as natural and instinctive to us both as it was for us to breathe. There could be no thought of marriage for us. I was still married, and any question of involvement in divorce proceedings would have ruined Philip's career. So, although in love, we could only be good, stanch companions. He brought the first touch of true romance into my life.

Some nights after the play Philip would come and fetch me and we would join a private party over at Rule's, the famous little restaurant in Maiden Lane, which plays such an interesting part in the theatrical history of London, just as the Cheshire Cheese in Fleet Street has always been associated with the literary and legal gentlemen of the city. The walls of Rule's were lined with signed photographs of actors and actresses, boxing champions, cabinet ministers, and racing figures, and the furnishings were still the same red-plush, gold-gilt chairs, china-globed chandeliers, and marble busts of Shakespeare and Sir Beerbohm Tree. The waiters were like "family retainers." They had served generations of British men of note, and while considering the wine list, it was quite the thing for them to advise: "Your father was always very partial to the Château Haut Brion, 1893, sir." The place was just the same as when Edward VII, then Prince of Wales, had given supper parties to Lily Langtry in the private room upstairs. This was the room in which we had our parties, and our young prince sat where his grandfather had sat, enjoying our gay chatter and the music, which came from the same old phonograph with its cylindrical records which stood on a marble pedestal in the corner.

One of the first things I did when I reached London in the summer of 1944 was to walk through Maiden Lane to see if Rule's was still standing. It was, and my heart bounded with joy that the Germans had not blasted that little bit of my past into dust and ashes. Rule's was closed and carefully shuttered. One hoped that its well-stocked cellar was carefully sandbagged, or that the precious bottles had been sent away into a less vulnerable part of England until the war was over. But the building was intact. It waited, as so many places in London seemed to wait, for England's youth and laughter to come back again. Meanwhile, Rule's kept guard over the memories of the many gay suppers we had had there.

I was often invited to the parties which the Prince of Wales gave in his apartment in St. James's Palace, at which everyone sang and danced and did stunts. These parties were always informal and entertaining. You met people of all sorts and from every walk of life and profession at the Prince's parties, but never anyone who was dull or stuffy. He invited international tennis champions, the newest blues singer, a guitarist who was all the rage in Paris, as well as his own intimate set. It was amusing that all this fun went on late at night inside the solemn old pile, with the sentries keeping up their march along the pavement just outside.

Whenever Philip came round to the theater to take me to one of the Prince's parties and our motor drove in at the gatehouse with the royal coat of arms over its portal, I always experienced a thrill. An unpretentious entrance led into the portion of the palace known as York House, which was occupied by the Prince just as it had been by his father when he was Duke of York. There was nothing elegant or stately about the Prince's private rooms—they were those of any well-off young bachelor who was interested in sports and in music. The Prince's bedroom might have belonged to any British schoolboy or an officer living in barracks. There was just a narrow, single iron bed with a table beside it on which there was always a glass of milk and an apple.

The Prince once took me on a tour of the state apartments in the palace. We paused at the window from which, according to the centuries-old tradition, every new sovereign is acclaimed on his accession to the throne. Each of us was thinking silently that someday the King's herald would proclaim from the balcony outside that very window: "The King is dead. Long live the King—Edward VIII." But I am sure neither of us suspected then how soon that was to happen, nor the cataclysmic events which were to bring about the abdication of Edward VIII. At that time, during the early twenties, no one in London had even heard of Mrs. Wallis Warfield Simpson.

In having his fling before settling down to the serious business which faced him ultimately, the Prince was giving England what the English people have always loved since the days of Prince Hal. As old George, the stage doorman at the theater, remarked with approbation: "Myself, I don't 'old with princes making parsons of theirselves. No, nor parsons and harchbishops setting theirselves up for lords." George was Labor and definitely anticlerical. He had a newspaper photograph of Ramsay MacDonald pasted on the wall above the backless old chair where he sat beside the stage door. But his political views in no way interfered with old George's truly British devotion to his King and the Royal Family. His feeling for them, if less reverent than Granny's, was no less loyal.

"Wot I say is, 'e's *'uman*. Even if Queen Victoria was his great-grandma."

With the coming of the summer I rented a small riverside cottage near Staines on the road to Windsor, and here I finally persuaded Mother, Dad, and Granny to take up residence with Pamela and me. It was near enough to London for me to get there every week end by train, and after a while Philip, who was stationed at Windsor, used to pick me up and take me home by car on his way back to barracks. Among our gay companions at that time was Lord Latham, and several times he and Philip and the others would stop at Buck's Club, pick up a hamper of chicken, fruit, champagne, et cetera, and we would all roar down to the cottage and get Mother out of bed to act as hostess. We would spread our feast al fresco over the dining-room table under the lamp with the silk fringe that hung from the ceiling.

One night we gave her a real surprise. We all arrived without warning, as usual, and routed her out of bed. Down she came, and we had supper. Suddenly she realized there was a stranger in our midst and that we were calling him "sir." Her gaze shot down the table, past his face, and fixed itself on my delighted grin; I nodded. I knew she had recognized the Prince of Wales. She then switched her gaze to Philip, and he smiled broadly. She was a triumph in her attempt to carry everything off without comment, and when the party was over, and as we stood at the gate saying good night, the Prince stretched out his hand to her. She curtsied and said, "Good night, Your Highness." I thought of those earlier days in Clapham: of how she always soared above debt and constant orders to dispossess. I put my arm around her as we went upstairs to peek at Pamela, and as I slipped into bed I grinned at her and said, "What about Cousin Ruby now, darling?"

André Charlot was planning a new revue to be called *A to Z*, in which Beatrice Lillie was to star with Jack Buchanan, Teddy Gerrard, and the Trix Sisters. I went down to the cottage to be with my baby and the family until something new should come along for me. Suddenly I got a telegram from Charlot saying that Beatrice Lillie was ill and that they had to open on a certain date. I went up to the theater, read the various sketches, heard the music, and signed up. Once more Beatrice Lillie's misfortune was the cause of my good fortune. From the opening night the revue was an enormous success. I sang "Limehouse Blues"; the orchestra was directed by Philip (Pa) Braham, who wrote the song with Douglas Furber. Jack Buchanan and I had wonderful material together, and Teddy Gerrard was a sensation.

A to Z was followed by another revue, *London Calling*, in which I was co-starred with Noel Coward and Maisie Gay. The show was written by Noel Coward, who had been cutting his teeth as a dramatist and actor. Noel floated back into my life exactly as if nothing had intervened between the days we were at Miss Conti's and the present. Noel is like that. He can disappear completely for years and then ring you up and continue the conversation you were having the last time you saw him.

The outstanding success of all Charlot's revues had brought him many offers from America. During the season of 1924 Archie Selwyn came to London, saw the revue, and arranged with Charlot to bring us to Broadway that winter. For the American edition Charlot made a conglomeration of popular numbers from all his revues. He signed on Bea Lillie, who had been doing a play of her own. She and I were to be featured as co-stars with Jack Buchanan and Herbert (Tommy) Mundin.

We sailed from Southampton on the last ship before Christmas, which meant that we traveled with a lot of Americans hurrying to get home for the holiday, as well as a number of British people who were going to be entertained at New York and at Palm Beach. We had a riotous trip. The instigator of most of the fun was Lord Beaverbrook. Alastair MacIntosh, who later married Constance Talmadge and who was the glamor boy of that year, was going home. Early in the trip Bea and Jack and I had confided to Allie our anxiety about where we were to stay in New York. It was the first time any of us had been there.

"Leave it to me, I'll fix the whole thing," said Allie with a grand gesture. "I'll send a radiogram to my friend William Rhinelander Stewart. He practically owns the Ambassador Hotel. He'll fix you up."

"Wonderful," Bea and I chorused. We left it at that.

Our ship docked on Christmas Eve. The long pier was a bedlam of porters, customs officials, reporters, and Americans welcoming home their friends and relatives. Suddenly Bea and I began to feel very lonely and strange. But Will Stewart was waiting at the gangplank. Jack, Bea, and I were finally driven to the Ambassador Hotel, where we were given two enormous suites—one for Jack and one for Bea and myself.

"So this is America!" I exclaimed. "Look at that bath, will you? Feel that delicious warmth. Central heating, my girl. No wonder they call this the most luxurious country on earth."

Bea stretched herself on her bed and sang ecstatically: "God bless Allie MacIntosh."

Next morning New York from our windows was wonderful. In the clear, sparkling air the tall white buildings were tremendously exciting. The view and the air made both of us ravenous. We ordered breakfast sent up. Presently there was a rap at the door. "Come in," Bea called. At that a procession of waiters, each pushing a little cart, advanced through the door in military formation. They wheeled the breakfast in to us, and such a breakfast—grapefruit, which we had never seen before, enthroned on shaved ice in silver bowls the size of washbasins; flagons of coffee and hot milk and cream; huge silver dishes under covers which the waiters whisked off with a flourish to reveal enormous slices of ham, toasted muffins, and God knows what all. "Take no notice," said Bea. "It's all done with mirrors." It was like a musical-comedy sketch only, as we discovered when the chief waiter ceremoniously presented us with the bill, the comic element was lacking. The bill was very real indeed, and for an amount that staggered us.

We were both still very hazy about the value of American money. I wasn't too sure of the value of the dollar in relation to the English pound. Bea lay back on her bed, pretended to be completely bored by the whole business, and said loftily, "Sign the check, darling, and give all the waiters a nice fat tip. Don't forget, it's Christmas."

This was no joke to me. "Come on, Bea," I said, "we've got to work this out and see how much we each owe, and how much we've got with which to pay it." We got out our purses and poured the contents onto the bed as soon as the waiters had gone.

Bea said, "It's perfectly simple. We each owe three dollars and fifty cents."

So we started to try to work it out, not knowing one piece of American money from another, until we laughed so hard that we were exhausted. When our laughter finally subsided, however, the seriousness of our position dawned upon us, and I said, "Let's call Jack and see if he's had breakfast."

A faint voice answered the telephone. "Yes, I've had breakfast, have you?"

"How much was yours?" I asked, and Jack replied, "It looks like three hundred and fifty shillings."

I relayed this to Bea and she said, "Tell him to come up here at once." He arrived, and we explained that he owed only three dollars and fifty cents, but that we were of the opinion that we were all in the wrong surroundings. After all, we were only in the rehearsal stage for the show—we might not be a success when we did open, and we had to have some money to get around with until then. "We'll have to get out of here at once," said Jack. Bea and I agreed. "But we must be dignified about it. Think of Will and Allie. They recommended us. How can we get out?"

Jack did some quick telephoning, got hold of Archie Selwyn, and explained our problem. We were recommended to Frank Case, who owns the Algonquin Hotel. Archie added: "And for God's sake, Jack, if you want to keep out of jail, don't let those dames sign any more checks."

As we were driving across town to our new hotel I suddenly saw what I took to be an enormous wild animal ambling down Fifth Avenue where we were stopped by a traffic light. I clutched Bea's arm.

"Look at that. What do you think it is?"

Bea peered out the window and began to laugh. She was born in Toronto and therefore not unaccustomed to the extraordinary sight of a six-foot man wearing a raccoon coat.

The light changed and the taxi shot across the Avenue and into Forty-fourth Street. Halfway along the block I exclaimed:

"There's that raccoon man again! How did he get here so quickly?"

Bea laughed again and explained.

"Do you actually mean there could be two of them in New York at once?" I demanded, awe-struck.

Within the next two days I was to learn that every undergraduate in town for the holidays was going about draped to the heels in shaggy skins, as though made up to play in *Androcles and the Lion.*

At the Algonquin Bea and I were given a room such as we might have had in the Midlands at home. The minute we looked around at the rather dark-figured wallpaper, the old-fashioned electric-light fixtures, the Brussels carpet, and the two brass beds with their crimson down-filled comforters, we said to each other: "This is more like it."

Before our New York opening, Bea and I were taken to see all the shows on Broadway. The boys rallied round to show us the town—Eddie Goulding, Billy Reardon, Allie, and Will Stewart. We soon lost that stranger-in-our-midst feeling that had come over us on the dock when our ship's companions flitted away and left Bea, Jack, and me sitting there with our luggage. We began to love New York.

12

Lillie and Lawrence,
Lawrence and Lillie,
If you haven't seen them,
You're perfectly silly.

ONE of the newspaper boys started singing that at a party one night to a tune of his own improvisation. This little ditty ran through our winter in New York with the persistence of a highly plugged theme song. But it was very complimentary, even if it wasn't good poetry, and it expressed some of the feeling—the gaiety, the nonsense, the lighthearted fun—which made *Charlot's Revue* unusual and memorable.

At least these were some of the things the New York critics said of the show when it opened at the Selwyn Theatre on New Year's Eve after a week's tryout in Atlantic City. "People" (and that included ourselves) who thought American audiences would never be amused by the English brand of humor were forced to think again when the *Revue*, which came originally for a six weeks' engagement, was held on for nine months. The critics—Heywood Broun, George Jean Nathan, Percy Hammond, Burns Mantle, Ring Lardner with Alexander Woollcott in the lead—gave their approval without qualification. These nabobs of the press were pleased with the potpourri Charlot had put together for them. They called each of us names—nice names. Their judgment had such a powerful influence on the American public that the show immediately became the outstanding smash hit of the season on Broadway and a "must" on everybody's list.

What seemed to impress the majority of critics was that the *Revue* was completely unlike any entertainment of its type ever given in New York heretofore. It is not difficult to explain the difference between *Charlot's Revue of 1924* and other musical shows, such as Ziegfeld's *Follies* and George White's *Scandals,* with which New Yorkers were familiar. Charlot's revues were characterized by an exquisite economy, a camaraderie between all the players and the audience such as had not been known in America up to this time. It was not a rough-and-ready intimacy, and never a jocular ad-libbing, but a mental closeness hard to define, and immediate in its appeal. His revues did not depend upon spectacular lighting and scenic effects for success. Most of the sketches were played against drapes, which were beautiful in themselves but not breath-taking. There was no spectacular electrical display. And no tremendous chorus, such as Ziegfeld and Earl Carroll featured in their productions. But every girl in the line had been selected to give an intimate individuality to the production.

"I do not engage an artist and then find a place for her," Charlot used to say. "First, I have the place; then I find the artist to fit it. I never buy names. What I pay for is personality, charm, talent." He certainly hadn't bought my name —he made it for me.

In place of the magical big names, gorgeous costumes advertised as costing hundreds of thousands of dollars, extraordinary mechanical effects, and much-featured show girls, the *Revue* depended for its success upon four principals backed by a well-picked small company, which gave a series of sketches, songs, and dances.

There was nothing bordering on the salacious in any of the acts. I think this proves conclusively that Americans and British alike welcome and will always support theatrical entertainment which is neither coarse, indecent, nor ribald.

As one American reviewer expressed it: "You don't have to be broad-minded to enjoy *Charlot's Revue*."

One of the high spots in the *Revue* was Bea Lillie's "March with Me" number, in which, dressed as Britannia, she led the line of girls, maintaining a very dignified and stiff demeanor while getting all tangled up with her feet and her props. Bea is one of those artists who are never any good at a rehearsal. She is a spontaneous comedienne. She needs the exhilaration of having an audience in front of her. Everyone who has ever worked with her knows this and knows that, though she is shy at rehearsals, she can be trusted to put her numbers over magnificently, and in her own inimitable way, when the moment comes.

But Archie Selwyn didn't know this when we were rehearsing for our New York opening. When he saw the "March with Me" number he shook his head over it. "When is she going to *show* me something?" he kept asking Charlot. And when Bea remained quiet and unresponsive, Archie declared the "March with Me" number, which had been a tremendous hit in London, would fall flat on Broadway. He tried to get Charlot to cut it from the show.

But Charlot knew his star. He refused to be budged an inch by Archie, and merely smiled blandly at all the gloomy prophecies; at even the two most direful words in theatrical parlance—"It stinks!"

And of course Charlot was right, as the opening night and every performance thereafter proved. Bea Lillie, as Britannia in "March with Me," was the outstanding hit of the *Revue*.

I had a number of sketches with Jack and Bea and Herbert Mundin, and I sang "Limehouse Blues" with Fred Leslie and Robert Hobbs. I also had a quiet little song called "I Don't Know" which caught on at once.

"Limehouse Blues" immediately became popular. We heard it in every night club in New York. In England we never plugged songs as they do in the United States, and I was surprised and extremely flattered to find everyone singing and playing "Limehouse" wherever I went. As a matter of fact they still do, after all these years.

I had a lot of things to learn about America and the American way of doing things; especially about the relative values of British and American expressions. I learned about these by the trial-and-error method.

Bea had been in America for a holiday when she married Robert Peel in 1922, but, like me, she knew nothing of the American theater or the reactions of American audiences. From the minute we landed until the night of our opening in New York I had gone around feeling as though someone had shot a hole through my middle; then, when we knew the show was a success and made the wonderful, exciting discovery that New Yorkers liked us, I felt suddenly like a colt in a pasture. My heels kicked up instinctively. I no longer walked, I pranced.

Determined to find out all we could about America, we went to all the plays we could crowd in, and on Sundays to the pictures.

Bea and I took a duplex apartment together in a converted house on West Fifty-fourth Street and this soon became a rendezvous for a gay crowd. Many of those who came there were connected, in one way or another, with the theater. There were composers, writers of lyrics, playwrights, and newspapermen. They would drop in at all hours, and it seemed to make no difference to them at all whether Bea or I was there. If we weren't, they would immediately make themselves comfortable and wait for one or the other of us to turn up.

We gave a lot of parties there. For one reason, it was such an easy thing to do. Whenever we gave parties, our friends would send us flowers, sometimes superb food from swanky restaurants and clubs, and a more-than-adequate supply of wines and spirits. William Rhinelander Stewart still hovered, and when spring came he sent a florist with orders to plant and maintain the garden at the rear of our apartment. And with the warm, sunny weather our parties moved out there. Our steady salonites included such grand people as Neysa McMein, Dorothy Parker, Jeanne Eagels, Bob Sherwood, Richard Barthelmess, Laurette Taylor, Will Stewart, Eddie McIlwain, Allie MacIntosh, George Ross, Charles Dillingham, Jimmie Walker, Aarons and Freedley, Ohman and Arden, Oscar Hammerstein, Howard Dietz, Arthur Schwartz, Jerome Kern, Irene Castle, Fanny Brice, June Walker, Estelle Winwood, Lenore Ulric, Billy Reardon, Irving Caesar and Vincent Youmans, Zez Confrey, Kallmer and Ruby, Rodgers and Hart, George and Ira

Gershwin, Irving Berlin, Jules Glaenzer, Clifton Webb, Prince Dmitri, Schuyler Parsons, Jascha Heifetz, Alexander Woollcott, and Eddie Goulding.

Alexander Woollcott quickly became one of our best friends. He used to frown and shake his big head and wiggle his fat forefinger in my face, like a schoolmaster.

"Young female, do you realize that you two girls have been feted over here as no visitors from overseas have been in the last twenty years?"

"I know!" I would look and feel very impressed. "But, Uncle Alexander, Americans are *so* enthusiastic. What's the Statue of Liberty for?"

Though I loved to tease Uncle Aleck and never could resist the temptation to do so, I valued his criticism and his praise whenever he saw fit to bestow either. He had—what is not at all rare in big, rather untidy men—unerring taste, and a sense of the delicacy of a situation. It pleased me no end when he said to me one day: "With no more than a pout, a twist of your shoulders, and two or three lines, you make me feel that I understand exactly how the wheels go round at the back of a girl's mind."

That, I knew, was a real tribute to Gertrude Lawrence the actress. Meanwhile, Gertrude Lawrence the woman savored the flattery of Percy Hammond's remark in his column: "It has been said of Miss Lawrence that every man in New York is, or was, in love with her."

So, without setting out to do it, Bea Lillie and I achieved the fame of being written up by the columnists, one of whom said, "Among the famous places to be visited in New York is the apartment of Beatrice Lillie and Gertrude Lawrence. *If you can get in.*"

As I look back over those mad, crowded months in New York, I cannot remember that Bea or I ever went to bed. Perhaps neither of us wanted to miss any of the fun, the laughter, and the music. People were always around. Scarcely a day went by that we weren't looked up by someone just over from London, who had dropped around the first thing to see us. During that summer the Prince of Wales came over for a visit to America before going on to his ranch in Canada. In his party, or following in its train, were a number of old friends of Bea's or mine, and they made our apartment their informal headquarters.

The piano in our apartment went all the time. Vincent Youmans was trying out new compositions. It never seemed to make any difference to him, or George Gershwin, that the conversation and laughter went on around him all the time and that no one paid the slightest attention to what he was doing. One might have thought this a most unfavorable atmosphere for the composition of musical scores, but as a matter of record Vincent Youmans and Irving Caesar wrote most of the score of *No, No, Nanette* in our living room, including "Tea for Two."

My friendship with George Gershwin and his brother Ira, which began that winter, was to develop into a wonderfully successful partnership when the brothers wrote the score and the lyrics of *Oh, Kay!* for me a year later. Gershwin was an assiduous worker and never spared himself. I remember going to hear his first performance of the "Rhapsody in Blue" at Aeolian Hall, and we met at a cocktail party at Condé Nast's afterward. George arrived late with every finger of both hands bandaged from the strain the rehearsals and first performance of the "Rhapsody" had demanded. He was a great man.

Of all the friends Bea and I made that winter, Jules Glaenzer was the most fabulous. He was the New York head of Cartier's and was famous for giving magical parties. He called us the Big Three—Lillie, Buchanan, and Lawrence.

Jules Glaenzer loved the theater and the theater folk loved him. Whenever I think of the parties at his house I always hear two or three pianos going at once. I think it can safely be said that more talent has been discovered in Jules Glaenzer's drawing room than anywhere else in New York, especially during the years of the middle twenties. Jules is one of those wonderful people, rare in any country and any society, who have great discrimination and who— though not artists themselves—are creative in their ability to encourage and develop artists of every sort. When he discovers a musician or a dancer or a painter, he is as thrilled over his find as if he had turned up a new and priceless gem.

I found American men extremely likable and flatteringly appreciative. Perhaps you have to be born an Englishwoman to realize how much attention American men shower on women and how tremendously considerate all the nice ones among them are of a woman's wishes.

It had been a surprise for us in the cast of *Charlot's Revue* to discover that the season on Broadway usually closed on June first, with a few shows running through the summer months. This, of course, was the exact reverse of things in London, where the season in the theater coincided with the "season" at Court and in society, which commences in May and continues until August bank holiday. So none of us had expected to stay on in New York through the summer. It was more or less generally understood that the *Revue* would close shortly before Easter and that we would sail for home to open in London when everyone would be in town. However, business on Broadway was so good that Archie Selwyn arranged with Charlot not only to hold the *Revue* over but to move to a larger theater, the Selwyn, next door. At the end of September we would start on a twenty weeks' tour, playing four weeks in Boston, two weeks in Philadelphia, four weeks in Chicago, and the major stands west of the Mississippi.

Our last night on Broadway was a fitting climax to the whole amazing nine months. The two front rows of the orchestra seats were taken by the columnists, critics, and celebrities of the theater. In fact, hardly anyone who was in the house that night was seeing the *Revue* for the first time. The majority of those in the audience knew our songs and sketches almost as well as we did, and their laughter and applause were not for the song or the sketch, but a personal and affectionate tribute to the actors. Bea's banjo voice and her famous index finger, which, as one reviewer put it, "was as elegant and uplifted as ever," were cheered as enthusiastically as if both were new to Broadway.

In one of Bea's numbers it was her custom to jump off the stage in fleeing from an Apache lover, and regain it again only after scrambling across the auditorium between the knees of those seated in the front row and the orchestra rail. At each performance Bea would drop unexpectedly into some man's lap. On closing night the lap she selected was Alexander Woollcott's very commodious one. We thought she would never get back onto the stage that night.

People were always telling us how surprised they were to find that the two women stars in the same show were good friends even to the point of living together. When we went into the Times Square Theatre, we found ourselves in adjoining dressing rooms, both of them small and stuffy. We asked to have the door removed between the two rooms. This allowed us to use one to dress in and the other for our visitors. It seemed to us a perfectly intelligent and not at all unusual way of arranging things, but we soon found that people were amazed by it, especially the manager of the show which was scheduled to follow us at that theater.

"Listen," he said, "the two dames in our show haven't spoken since we opened. That door will have to be closed up between them rooms or there'll be murder."

On our closing night, after the finale, the whole house stood up and cheered us. They pelted us with flowers. When the orchestra struck up "Auld Lang Syne" the audience and company joined in the singing. Everyone took hold of the hand of the person next to him. The chain of friendly handclasps stretched across the stage, across the footlights, and continued through the house.

When the audience was finally pushed out of the theater several hundred of them merely adjourned to the stage door, where they formed such an imposing mob scene that traffic was clogged in Forty-second Street.

When Bea and I came out, laden with flowers, to get into our waiting taxi, we found the roof of the vehicle packed with the more ardent revelers, who escorted us through the streets of New York singing our own songs to us.

13

WHEN WE CLOSED in New York we went to play Boston. I very nearly said to play Harvard College, because the house was sold out night after night to Harvard students, many of whom had already seen the show in New York several times over, and had come backstage and were friends of the cast. Johnny Green was one of them.

Johnny came round to my dressing room the night before we closed in Boston to take me out to supper.

"I can't go," I told him. "I'm ill. I have a terrible cold."

It was true. I had been fending off a cold for several weeks, and as soon as we reached Boston the climate there had overcome all my efforts. I was feverish and hoarse and shivering miserably. Johnny looked me over critically.

"By rights, you should be home and in bed," he said.

"That's exactly where I'm going," I told him. "I'd like to crawl into bed and stay there for a week." The thought of having to play two shows the next day made me feel limp.

"Oh, I'll get you over it," Johnny offered. "Do you know the best way to cure a cold instantly?"

"No. How?"

"Castor oil."

"I'd rather die, thank you."

"I'll show you a way so you'll never taste it." And when I looked at him doubtfully, he added, "All the fellows take it that way. It is one of the things you learn at Harvard."

I agreed to let Johnny dose me, and he took me home to the hotel and ordered up a terrifying quantity of castor oil and half a dozen bottles of sarsaparilla. "What's the sarsaparilla for?" I demanded suspiciously.

"You'll find out," said Johnny, and began, with a bartender's gestures, to shake up a fizz of oil and sarsaparilla.

"Now, toss that off!"

I downed the nauseating mixture and made a face.

"You British are decidedly effete," said Johnny patronizingly. "Undoubtedly the best blood of England came over on the *Mayflower*. The ones the Pilgrim Fathers left behind simply didn't have the stamina."

"Oh! Didn't we!" Between the kidding and the castor oil my temper was rising. My eye lighted on the bulky case on top of one of my trunks. In it was the saxophone Johnny was teaching me to play. I took the sax out of its case and blew a wailing note.

"My God, it sounds like a French taxicab," he cried.

(I found out in 1929 that those discordant notes on the saxophone were the inspiration for one of Johnny's greatest song hits, "Body and Soul." I took the song to England with me and later I gave it to Libby Holman.)

I glared at him and put all my efforts into what I hoped would be a rousing rendition of "God Save the King." I sounded most of the notes, but a few were squeaky and others trailed off forlornly. The more Johnny grinned, the more determined I was to play my national anthem, so I kept at it.

"Ah yes," said Johnny reminiscently, " 'America.' I know that number too." And to my accompaniment he began to sing unfamiliar words that had to do with the scenery of the United States. I tried to drown out his singing with the sax. All at once I began to feel very peculiar.

> *"Let music swell the breeze,*
> *And ring from all the trees*
> *Sweet freedom's song . . ."*

thundered Johnny.

"S-Q-A-A-A-K," went the saxophone. It dropped between my knees and I tumbled over it. Johnny gathered me up and carried me into the bathroom, where I proceeded to be thoroughly and embarrassingly sick.

He had the effrontery to look pleased with the whole proceeding, and when he had helped me back into my bed and covered me up with all the blankets available the wretch congratulated me on my fine performance. "You'll wake up in the morning and never know you had a cold," he assured me. "That's the way we do things at Harvard."

Maybe that drastic treatment works wonders on the students at Harvard College. It failed with me. I was ill and miserable all next day, though I managed to drag myself through the two performances. When the company left for Toronto, I felt like something the cat had dragged home, and whenever Charlot looked at me there was a little worried frown between his eyes. My voice was hoarser than ever, and I was definitely lightheaded.

Toronto was Bea's home town and welcomed us with open arms. The house was sold out right through our stay there, and parties were scheduled for every night. I didn't want to seem a spoilsport, so I kept going though I alternately shivered and burned with fever.

On Thursday evening Bea Lillie said to me: "There's a man here I used to be engaged to as a kid. He's giving a party for us tonight at his house."

I said I thought I wouldn't go.

"Oh, darling, you mustn't miss it," said Bea. "It's sure to be lots of fun. They are coming for us in a car. We needn't stay long."

"Very well," I replied.

After the performance we motored to our host's house outside the city where about twenty people were waiting for us in a big living room. My head was throbbing, and I was cold all over. I got into a big chair as close to the fire as I could and basked in its warmth. I had taken several aspirins before I left the theater. I was aware that my chest hurt, but for some unexplainable reason these things no longer mattered. They were happening to someone who was no longer I. Presently we all went into the dining room to supper. Out of the mist that surrounded me appeared a short, slight elderly man who smiled and whispered:

"I've been to see your play tonight. My dear, you have the heart of a bullock, but you are riding for a fall. Take care."

I tried to toss off some light rejoinder. "Silly little old man," I thought. "He looks like 'Mr. Pim Passes By!'"

As though in response to my thought, he floated away again into the mist and was replaced by other figures. There were so many I began to feel dizzy. "I don't feel well," I said suddenly. "Please, won't someone take me home?" Someone apparently did, though I was past being aware of who it was. All I knew was that presently I was in my bed—and drifting off to sleep.

Suddenly I woke. I switched on the light. Four o'clock. I looked around my room. Everything in it was familiar, but everything was about four times the size it should have been. I felt like Alice in Wonderland. I crawled out of bed and looked into Bea's room, which adjoined mine. Bea had not come in yet.

I found the thermometer that I carried in my dressing case and tried to find out if I had a temperature. The figures on the little glass stick read 104 degrees. "That can't be right," I thought. "No one can have a temperature of 104 degrees." I crept back into bed and closed my throbbing eyes.

I must have dozed again, for when I woke it was five o'clock. Again I took my temperature—104 degrees. "What a silly thermometer." I got up and went into Bea's room. She was in bed, sleeping peacefully, but I woke her.

"Bea," I mumbled, and my voice came from miles away, "do you know how to take a temperature?"

Bea yawned while I held the tube under my tongue for a minute; then she blinked at the figures. "One hundred and four!" she said in an awed tone.

"That's what it said before," I told her. "Bea, what happens when you have a temperature of 104 degrees?"

"You die," said Bea. "Get back into bed, darling. I'm going to call a doctor."

Meekly I obeyed. Everything became even more out of proportion. I felt I was living in a dream, and this seemed all the more credible when suddenly there appeared at my bedside the same kindly old gentleman I had met that evening at the party. "Didn't I tell you so?" he remarked, but not crossly. Then he proceeded to give orders to the nurses who appeared as if by magic, and I was rolled in blankets and carried downstairs, stuffed into an ambulance, and motored away to Wellesley Hospital. I heard someone say, "Double pneumonia." Another voice said, "Pleurisy." Someone else said, "Dr. Ross is in charge of the case."

I did not know when the *Revue* closed in Toronto and the company went on to its next date, leaving me behind. I didn't know that there were stories in all the newspapers, telling that Gertrude Lawrence was desperately ill. Or that a photograph of me in a hospital bed, and looking as though I already had one foot in the grave, appeared in a London paper where Mother saw it and nearly died of shock. I didn't know anything at all until one day I opened my eyes and found myself lying, literally embowered in flowers. Bewildering sprays of forsythia, dogwood, and lilac covered the walls. Baskets of roses and lilies were banked against these, and there was an enchanting, fully trimmed Christmas tree in the corner. The last words I remembered hearing Bea Lillie say flashed through my mind:

"When you have a temperature of 104 degrees, you die."

"So I'm dead," I thought. "It's not bad at all. I feel like *La Dame aux Camellias.*"

It was while I lay in Wellesley Hospital in Toronto that I first realized there was something wonderful in being somebody. There in the hospital, with no member of my family or even an old friend near me, I made the discovery that, through caring about my work, people had come to care about me when I was ill, and this was deeply satisfying. All the telegrams, cablegrams, and letters which poured into the hospital from people in the United States and at home, all the flowers and messages and other gifts from people who were complete strangers to me and who knew me only as an actress who had entertained them, and even the stupendous floral offerings of Mr. Ziegfeld which arrived from New York packed in ice and at regular intervals—all these were proof positive. They were a beautiful way of saying "thank you" for the gift of laughter. They were the rewards for hours of rehearsal and hard work, and the schooling of André Charlot.

I had apparently been very ill—had had transfusions—and missed Christmas, hence the tree.

I was ill for fourteen weeks. Toward the end of that time Philip Astley came over from England and stayed in Toronto so he could visit me. As soon as Dr. Ross said I could be moved, a nurse was engaged and Philip took us to New York and right aboard ship. Dr. Ross had ordered me to take a long rest in the sun and approved Philip's suggestion of taking me to stay with mutual friends who had a villa on the Riviera.

As soon as I was able, we motored about the Riviera and over the border into Italy and far into Sicily. We went sight-seeing in mellow old temples, and we lived where the garden walls were hung with wistaria and amid lemon and orange and olive blossoms—the most romantic stage drop I ever played against. How lucky I was to have seen all that beauty before its destruction by this war.

Charlot cabled us that the company was scheduled to sail from New York. Philip motored me from Italy up to Cherbourg to meet the ship, and there I rejoined Bea, Tommy, Charlot, and the company, and went on with them to England to be ready to open at the Prince of Wales Theatre in the "Triumphant return from America of *Charlot's Revue.*"

14

FROM CATTERICK our E.N.S.A. caravan took the road to the north with Glasgow as our ultimate destination, but when we arrived in Newcastle the first night, we found orders to drive back forty miles along the way we had come to put on a concert at Barnard Castle for the Tank Corps. We were all pretty "browned off" by then, as we had had no rest, no food, and we were faced with the forty-mile ride back to Newcastle after the show. Eighty miles to give one half-hour show. It was lucky all of us were veteran troupers, experienced in playing one-night stands. There is no room for a prima donna and no field for the prima-donna temperament on a camp tour.

When I first joined up with the others I was aware that they watched me narrowly. They wondered if I could take it. That made me smile. Hadn't I been a trouper myself for years? I knew all the discomforts of being on the road—at least I thought I did. I was to find that playing the camps in wartime is quite different from playing theaters—even small ones—during peace.

But those furtive, wary glances reminded me of the time I made a film at Paramount's Long Island studio. I had just finished starring in *Candle-Light*. I hadn't been working at the studio for more than a few days before I realized everyone was waiting for me to blow up and be temperamental. When I did not, I got the feeling I had failed to live up to expectations; failed to behave as a star was popularly supposed to behave.

Our unit was one of the lucky ones, with no personality to sound a sour note. After weeks of touring together, we had settled down into a good working company. Each of us could appreciate, through experience, the qualities of all the others.

Big, blonde Zoë Monte, who sang sentimental ballads in a high, astonishingly true soprano, and her husband, Basil Melford, were our double act. Zoë and Basil had been married for twenty-five years and were devoted to each other. She looked after him and mothered him, which he pretended to rebel against, but obviously couldn't have done without.

Clarence Myerscough's orchestra was one of our attractions. Clarence is a Lancashireman, but from studying and appearing for years abroad he has lost his Lancashire burr and now owns an accent which has become so perfect I thought he could have come only from Vienna. The Viennese note suited Clarence amazingly. In fact, it suited him so perfectly that I think even he, as well as everyone else, had forgotten it was not real. Later on we were to be very grateful for his knowledge of French—especially the patois.

A third act was supplied by Wilfred Hubbard and his "fifty-two assistants"—a pack of cards. Wilfred's tricks were a never-ending amazement to us in the unit as well as to the audiences.

Our accompanist, May, was Irish—innocent, vague, and a darling. Stanley Kilburn was our pianist, and a very brilliant one. Stanley had ulcers of the stomach which Mary Barrett, who shepherded all of us, undertook to cure. I think Mary's chief concern during our tour was to keep me happy and at the top of my form and to return Stanley to London headquarters minus his ulcers. Mary's real boss was Gracie Fields, about whom she had a ceaseless fund of stories. Fortunately, she and all the other members of the unit were endowed with that priceless ingredient for making an adventure go over—a sense of humor. We were often able to laugh about things that happened to us en route, which, in different company, would have been annoying and infuriating.

I was thinking of this during the short stay we made in Edinburgh. I hadn't been in the hotel five minutes when a dour-looking man, whom I noticed standing in the lobby, came over to our group and addressed himself to me. "Do ye ken are there any E.N.S.A. shows in Edinburgh the noo?"

I said I didn't know of any. "Why?"

He drew down his overlong upper lip with great seriousness. His voice dropped confidentially. "Did you no' hear aboot the trouble over at Ballycraig?"

"No," I replied.

"The wee bairns threw stones at the actors."

"Why did they do that?" I asked.

"Happen they didna like them." He smacked his lips. "We Scots are vurra particular."

"So I've heard," I said pacifically. "As a matter of fact, our E.N.S.A. troupe has played to a good many Scottish soldiers. And I've played in Edinburgh myself. Nothing like that has happened to me."

"Nay," he said. "But ye can neverrr tell when it might, lassie. So take this wee pamphlet." He handed me a tract with the alarming title: TAKE HEED, FOR THE END DRAWETH NIGH. And with that walked away.

Though we weren't stoned anywhere by the particular Scots, we had encountered a sufficient number of difficulties before we landed in Edinburgh. For instance, when we arrived at Dundonald, outside Glasgow, to put on our show, we found that the coach with all the costumes and the musicians' dress suits and instruments was missing. We postponed the show for an hour. When that passed and still no coach had arrived, Stanley, the pianist, Clarence—who always carried his violin in his lap while traveling—and I started a sort of impromptu show of our own and kept things going until the costumes did arrive and the others were ready. Around 10:00 P.M. our real show opened. We rang down at eleven forty-five, dog-tired, but knowing we hadn't failed the boys, and happy in their applause. We were invited to go to the mess for a drink, which we did and were glad of—no food though. Then we motored back the thirty-five miles to Glasgow, only to find that the hotel had fed our suppers to some hungry sailors and had bedded down a number of the jack-tars in our bedrooms. By doubling up, however, we managed to get some sleep.

When we set out from London for the north, it was with the definite promise that, having played the camps en route, our unit would then be sent on to the Orkneys. As everyone knew, though the censorship jealously guarded news from that terrifically important naval base, the Fleet put in and out of Scapa Flow. Since that censorship still holds, I am constrained to tell only briefly the story of our tour of this advanced post.

We left our motorized equipment in Edinburgh to fly over the Highlands and the narrow but tempestuous Pentland Firth which divides the Orkneys from John o' Groats. The Firth is only six to eight miles across, but it has a bad reputation for its dangerous currents, and I was more than glad that we were to fly over it. The flight north from Edinburgh was wonderful, though we ran through alternate rainstorms, sunshine, and mists. This, of course, was the country to which, in happier days, Philip and his friends went regularly every twelfth of August for the grouse shooting. Nothing short of a broken back could have caused Philip not to keep his annual August engagement with the Scotch grouse.

We were driven to our billets in Kirkwall, which is the largest town in the islands, just a mile or two from Scapa. The place had been built as a hotel for anglers and vacationists; then came the war, and the Navy took it over for billets. I had my first bath in three days, then dropped into bed and slept like a child.

The place was like a barracks, and full of WRENS, WAAFS, soldiers, sailors, marines, and their wives and children. At 6:00 A.M. the sergeant in charge tramped down the corridor and banged on the door of every room with an iron ladle, of all things, until the occupant replied, thereby giving evidence he or she was awake. I was up and out early, relishing the brisk salt breeze.

We were invited to lunch with Admiral Sir Henry Moore aboard the flagship H.M.S. *Duke of York*. Afterward his launch took us to our permanent billets on the island of Flotta. Here E.N.S.A. had its own hut, just like an army Nissen hut, except it was made of wood. The eighteen members of our unit crowded the hut almost to bursting. The girls shared three rooms, and the boys had one large one at the end of the hut, with me in a single in the middle. The nights were cold, with high winds. We used to collect driftwood to burn in the coke stove while we got ready for bed. All our journeys had to be made by "drifter." It was fun going out, but the return trips were uncomfortable, long, and cold.

It was amazing on this isolated, bleak, treeless reef, with its entanglements of barbed wire, to find a fine theater— good stage, dressing rooms, and excellent acoustics. And of course the most appreciative audiences in the world. The men were either stationed here for the duration and sealed in or they had come in from the sea, veterans of many tough battles.

We shoved off about 1:00 P.M. in a drifter for the garden spot of the Orkneys, which is a little island called South Ronaldsay. Its port has the lovely name of St. Margaret's Hope. We went aboard to a stiff breeze, a good swell, and a strong smell of frying fish. Mary Barrett immediately nosed out the galley and saw to it that a half kipper was passed out to all of us. As we had an hour's trip ahead of us to St. Margaret's Hope, the smell of the crew's mess and the sample we had of it were maddening. How do men live for days and days at sea without food and water? Then, as if in answer to my hunger pangs, a head popped up the galley steps from below and a voice said: "Yer tea's ready."

We girls—Zoë, Joan, May, Mary, and I—went below and had the most wonderful meal with the skipper and his three mates. Great mugs of ship's tea, huge slices of bread thickly spread with butter and jam, and a dish of kippers *cooked in butter!* After we had eaten our fill, the men of our unit were invited down to be fed.

The drifter's crew did this for us voluntarily, and the only way we could show our appreciation was to see that they were all invited to the show we put on that night. One of our most appreciative observers was the Bishop of Edinburgh, who was visiting the flagship and sat in the front row and laughed louder than any of the sailors, although I think he had his gentle doubts about the merits of "I Wanna Get Married."

This life is certainly one of ups and downs—one day tea and kippers with the drifter's crew, the next, dinner with Sir Henry and Lady Harwood at Malsetta House, which is the Government House of the Orkneys. The first intimation I had of being introduced into this atmosphere of gold braid and good breeding was the message that Sir Henry and Lady Harwood would like to meet me, and please would I call at Malsetta House on my way to the show. I thought this a bit odd, as I had known Sir Henry when he was on the *Exeter* and before he was knighted for sinking the *Graf Spee*. However, the Malsetta House car met us at the pier at Hoy and drove Mary and me ten miles to be greeted by a house party of twelve people. Lady Harwood said: "Hello, my dear. Would you like to go straight to your room or will I just send your bag up?"

I said that I was going to dress at the theater, at which Sir Henry cut in: "But you're dining and staying the night with us, as your shows are on this side tomorrow."

I stood dumfounded in my trench coat and khaki uniform. Mary coughed. We were an hour's boat journey away from headquarters and our bags.

"I have a lovely fire in your bedroom. We shall be *so* disappointed if you don't stay."

The thought of a bedroom with a fire in it, even just to look at, was bliss, so I accepted the invitation to dinner. Mary and I used the Malsetta bathroom, sat by the fire in the bedroom, and then went downstairs.

We went in to dinner—all very grand, with menservants to wait on us, and we had delicious fresh-caught salmon. It was getting late, and I began to look questioningly at Mary. We had to drive ten miles to the show and I had to make up. My mind was wandering, and in my abstraction I refused the port. The steward filled my wineglass with water; then I realized too late we were about to toast the King!

I stood with the commander of the Fleet and drank the toast to His Majesty *in water,* and felt like some miserable figure in a Bateman drawing!

For upward of ten days we did the Orkneys, putting on shows aboard ships like H.M.S. *Dundas Castle*, which was a ghost ship of the good old days of pleasure cruises. The *Dundas Castle* used to sail to Africa with tourists and passé actors making farewell tours. She was about to be broken up for scrap in 1938 when the Navy took her over and remodeled her into the maid-of-all-work to the Fleet.

Her engineers repair the ships that put in for repairs. Her dentist, Dr. Gamble, fills all the aching cavities that come his way. Officers awaiting leave, or returning from leave, are quartered aboard her until they can rejoin their own ships. She handles all the mail for the Fleet in Scapa Flow. Her theater, down in her bowels, far below sea level, has to be seen to be believed. You go down a million stairs and suddenly come upon an auditorium with red plush tip-up seats, a real stage, and good dressing rooms. All these were part of the cinema which was the attraction of B deck when the *Castle* was a pleasure-cruise ship.

On our last day at work in the Orkneys we left by drifter for the island of Shapinsay to do our last show for the Navy. There were only about three hundred men and two officers in the camp, and most of them had been there without leave for a long time. Shapinsay is much too small and too remote —though terribly important in the chain of defenses—to be on the list for E.N.S.A. shows to visit. Ours was the first star unit to go there. All the villagers and their children were admitted to the show.

When we left Shapinsay around five-thirty in the afternoon, we cajoled the skipper into giving us a long-way-round trip home to our billets in Kirkwall. None of us looked forward with any eagerness to another night on a NAAFI cot, such as we had been sleeping on in the hostels. The prevailing knobbiness of the thin mattresses made one feel one was curled up on a sack of coals.

We had been invited to spend our last evening in the sergeants' mess at Kirkwall, and we all looked forward to a rousing good time. On the way there I was asked to drop in to see the new Arts Club, which had been opened in the town. When we drove round, there was a group of people waiting by the door. A naval officer detached himself from the group to greet us and escort us inside, where I found myself suddenly standing beside a grand piano and heard the officer announce: "And now it gives me great pleasure to present Miss Gertrude Lawrence, the celebrated stage and film star."

To my horror, I saw a room vaguely filled with elderly women, young girls, and a few shy naval officers. One very mannish-looking female had a hearing device placed on the table before her, connected by a long cord to her ear which, presumably, wired her for sound.

I stood there in the midst of this truly Noel Coward setting and said: "Thank you so much," and was about to sit down when the Navy man whispered, "What shall I announce you are going to sing?"

I was trapped. I had not suspected the reason of our visit to the Arts Club, and my pianist had no music with him. However, he went to the piano and played a few chords and I sang "I Wanna Get Married." This drew repressed giggles from the girls and frozen silence from the older listeners. The female who reminded me of a Helen Hokinson drawing, however, seemed delirious with joy. This led me to wonder if she was the only human being in the club or if her ear gadget had not been tuned in and she was merely trying to be polite, not having heard a word.

After the song I sat down, feeling that I was awaiting sentence. Then Stanley was invited to play. He was very angry, but his humor rose above his wrath, so he played with a great deal of bravado and many sour notes.

After the tepid applause, someone said: "Let's have some choruses." Stanley obliged again, and our audience sang them in a refined, having-a-hell-of-a-time, let's-all-be-devils sort of way.

After this we left, but not until the three naval officers had come up and apologized because the club had no bar. We said it was quite all right and that the club was charming and that we didn't drink anyway, so we left.

Well, the sergeants' mess, when we arrived there, liberally made up for this deficiency. We had an impromptu show which ended in a supper of large plates of fresh shellfish and beer.

When the barkeep showed signs of wearying, I offered to take his place.

"This is a ticklish sort of job," he said, trying to put me off.

"Let me show you how well I can do it," I begged him.

He agreed to this, and let me draw a couple of mugs.

"I must sye, you do very well for a hamachoor."

"Amateur nothing, Sergeant! I was a barmaid myself once. Earned my keep at it, too, for several weeks. And built up custom too."

The sergeant gave me a look which could be interpreted as "The hell you were!" But he said with an effort toward politeness, "Maybe in a play, in the theayter."

"Not in a theater; at the Red Lion Hotel in Shrewsbury."

To him I was a star, and, like most simple folk, he probably thought I always had been.

It was quite true, that bit about my having been a barmaid. It came about in this way: One of the touring companies I was playing in, before I had my chance in *André Charlot's Revue*, played Shrewsbury. Three of us girls put up at the Red Lion, which gave special rates to theatricals. Shrewsbury is a busy county town, and the Shropshire farmers who drove in on market day had a way of dropping into the Lion for a glass of Shrewsbury ale. They were not amiss to getting a glimpse of a pretty face, a mass of curls, and a winning smile along with their drinks.

Our company manager at the time was a little man with a

strawberry nose and very thick lenses. We all called him "Old Four Eyes."

Anything could happen in such tacky little shows in those days, but we were not prepared for what was in store for us this time. Saturday came and we played the matinee and waited for the manager to appear with the salaries. But "Old Four Eyes" had flown the coop with the takings.

We three girls returned gloomily to the Red Lion and discussed what was to be done. As usual, we had very little money between us. I had not enough to pay my week's lodging at the inn. As I thought of my wardrobe, which consisted chiefly of props, I put far from me the idea that I could pawn any of it for sufficient money to take me back to London to hunt a new job.

The other girls were more solvent than I. They were able to pay what they owed at the Lion. One of them had enough money to take her to London. The other, Myrtle, had a sister married to a stationer in Birmingham and near enough to be a refuge during this emergency.

"Not that I shall be welcome," Myrtle said. "Her old man never did cotton to me. It was one of those marriages. Percy's family are highly respectable, I'd have you know, and what *they* think of theatricals isn't fit for any girl's ears."

"How are you going to explain to them when you arrive?" I wanted to know.

Myrtle gave me a wink over her plump, bare shoulder. "Trust Sis and me. We'll think of something to tell Percy. Later I'll get to London somehow."

As far as I could see, I would have to remain in Shrewsbury—alone and on my own. At least until something turned up for me somewhere. The Theatre Royal in Shrewsbury was a place on the regular route of many of the companies which played the provinces and, not infrequently, as I knew, a company on tour counted on picking up someone to fill a minor part in each town they played. This arrangement was usually cheaper than carrying a regular performer for the part, and it brought business, because all the girl's family and friends would come to see her. Perhaps some such stroke of luck would come my way if I waited long enough. But, in the meanwhile, there were my expenses at the inn. I was puzzling over a way of meeting these when Myrtle turned around from her mirror.

"I don't like leaving you here, kiddo," she said.

"Oh, I'll be all right," I hastened to assure her. "I have a plan."

And I had. The idea had come to me as an inspiration. I refused to tell Myrtle, but my repeated assurance that I was not altogether without resources cheered her tremendously.

I went downstairs next morning and asked to see the proprietor of the Red Lion. I was under no necessity to explain to him what had happened to our company, for he knew. To him I appealed with disarming candor. I was stony, and I was not denying it. I owed his inn in the neighborhood of twenty-seven shillings; but, I hastened to assure him, I would welcome the chance to pay the indebtedness by working.

"What can you do?"

"I could work in the bar."

His eye went over my head in the direction of the taproom where his regular barmaid, a large, blowzy girl, named—ironically—Tina, was lazily polishing glasses. From Tina the landlord's eye came back to rest on me.

"I could do with another girl in the bar," he said thoughtfully. "The only difficulty is . . ."

"I know," I said quickly. "Tina."

He nodded. "Tina's a good girl. She's been with me three years. She's a cousin of my wife's. Knows all the steady customers and what each one of them likes. Can give 'em back as good as they give her too."

"Suppose you leave Tina to me," I suggested. "She'll understand I'm not here to take her job away from her—only to help her through the busy season."

That bit about the busy season was carefully planted. It was August, and the annual Shrewsbury Floral and Musical Fete was scheduled for Wednesday and Thursday of the following week.

In the end, the landlord took me on. He led me up to Tina and announced with bluff good humor that, in view of the warm weather and the increased customers which the fete was sure to bring, he had engaged me as her assistant. I ran upstairs and broke the news to the girls. They came down and drank a glass of port on the house. Then they left for their trains. I was now a barmaid.

At first Tina was inclined to be suspicious of me and my intentions. It was a decided novelty for a chorus girl to turn barmaid, and Tina could not believe that I was doing this without ulterior motives. I made a clean breast to her of my situation, and because she was kindhearted she laid aside her original suspicions. Generously she lent me a dozen kid curlers and showed me how to put up my hair on them so I should have the mop of curls which used to be considered part of a barmaid's make-up.

When I entertained her with tales of my experiences and

anecdotes of other actors and actresses—some of whom she had seen—she became my friend. She even approved of my way of polishing the glasses and shining the pewter beer taps. After two days she let me do all of it. In return, she taught me how to draw a full, yet not overflowing, glass of beer. This, as the barkeep at the sergeants' mess at Kirkwall was to tell me many years later, is something no amateur can do. Thanks to Tina—and the busy season in Shrewsbury —I am a professional at it.

I was a success as a barmaid, if I do say it. The regular customers—the commercial travelers, farmers, and tradesmen from the shops—seemed to welcome the novelty of a new barmaid who sang as she drew them a drop of what they fancied. Business at the Red Lion was brisk.

What with my wages and tips I paid off my debt to the landlord and managed to set aside something to stand me in good stead when my opportunity came. It came, ultimately, with a company which opened at the Shrewsbury Theatre in a dramatic play called *The Rosary*. The management wanted a local girl and, thanks to my success in the bar at the Lion, the manager had not been in town an hour before he was told by someone to stop round at our place, have a glass of dark and bitter, and look me over. I was engaged to dress as a nun and sing the song "My Rosary" as a prologue to the play to give it "atmosphere"!

My return to the profession was celebrated in the taproom of the Lion, and the manager was congratulated on his choice. Though the annual fete was over, our customers did not fall off, for the simple reason that a number of citizens and quite a few of the masters and boys from Shrewsbury's celebrated public school came there on the chance of being served by the girl they had just seen in the play at the theater. This might have turned the tide of my fortunes in such a direction that I would have remained behind bars all my life, but fortunately for me the publicity worked as well in the opposite direction. People came to the theater in order to see the nun who was barmaid at the Red Lion.

When the company left Shrewsbury for its next stand, I paid my bill at the Red Lion and returned to London, the Cats' Home, and the casting offices. It is a matter of pride to me that the landlord remarked on our parting, "Gertie, you can have a job here in my bar any time."

15

I THINK everyone felt a little sad when it came time to fly away from the Orkneys.

We arrived at Donnibristle in time for tea—three planes full—including trunks, drums, double basses, and Zoë. May was scared during the flight, which we made in wonderful weather, but everyone came through without mishap until just before landing, when Harry, the saxophone player, was suddenly sick from sheer relief that the flight was over.

We put on a show for the Fleet Air Arm at seven-thirty, then caught the ten-thirty ferry across the Forth and slept that night at Hawes's Inn, under the shadow of the famous bridge and the eagle eyes of the M.P.s. As a rule, no one was allowed to break a journey at this point, either going in or out of Edinburgh, as one attempt was made by the Germans to destroy the bridge, and the area was under heavy guard. Since we were traveling under military orders, an exception was made for us.

Our next stop was in a small Cumberland village, and was occasioned by no less a demand than our hunger for the fish and chips we smelled frying in a little shop. Four of us sat on the running board of the truck and ate that greatest of all English delicacies out of newspaper. It was the first time I had had that treat of my childhood in many years and I found my appetite for it undiminished.

Mary told us a true story of a five-months-old baby who was brought into one of the London day nurseries. The family had not had a drop of milk for many weeks. Asked how they had managed to feed the baby, the mother replied: "We gave her a little bit of whatever we had."

What they had was principally fish and chips, washed down by strong tea. The fact that the baby had survived this diet would seem to prove that forty-eight million Britishers can't be wrong.

Our first job in Manchester, at nine-thirty next morning, was to rehearse for a monster broadcast from Belle Vue, the amusement park. I worked all day, broke long enough to have my picture taken riding Lil, the elephant, and another in a hair-raising roundabout known as the Caterpillar. The last time I did that stunt was in 1937 with Douglas, now Lieutenant Commander, Fairbanks.

The crowd at the broadcast was enormous—eight thousand servicemen present, and very thrilling.

Basil Dean came down from London for the show, recalling to me the fact that the first time I ever played in Manchester was under his direction. He introduced me with words that gave me a shock: "Miss Gertrude Lawrence, who is now on her way to Normandy."

Basil had just returned from Bayeux, where he had been making plans to send the first E.N.S.A. units into France.

This was my first official notice that I was to be allowed to go across to the invasion front, for which we had seen so many men set out. It was what I had hoped for, begged for, worked for—the opportunity to entertain the fighting men at the actual front.

At that moment I was glad of every springless, lumpy

camp bed I had stretched my weary bones upon. It had all been our basic training.

We signed our papers before we left Manchester and received our orders to proceed to London for inoculations as soon as our tour ended—in less than a week.

During the next six days we literally raced across England, doing shows for the Navy and the Air Force and the WAAFS. At St. Nathan's Camp, near Cardiff, twenty-four hundred airmen and WAAFS packed themselves into a theater only big enough to hold fourteen hundred. The audience was, literally, two deep. St. Nathan's, I was told, was the largest air-training camp in the world, with a personnel of forty thousand. Our unit would have had to stay there a week and give two shows a day to entertain that audience.

We ran on south into the invasion area and all the bustle and turmoil again. The sky above us was full of planes, bearing other glider planes with air-borne troops, towed by the famous nylon-stocking line. The roads were jammed with trucks and tanks and soldiers of all the services— literally millions of men and mountains of ammunition—all headed one way—to France.

So we came at last to Salisbury in the shadow of the famous cathedral, which was still intact and strangely serene in the martial atmosphere that filled the old town. We did a show for the Army at Lark Hill Camp. Our last two shows in this area, under canvas at Bustard Camp and for the R.A.F. at Keevil, gave me a taste of what I was told I could expect across the Channel. Our stage was improvised out of kitchen tables, and the lighting was done with hastily rigged kerosene lamps. Afterward, in the mess where we were given supper, the rats came out and eyed us hungrily as we gobbled our Spam and salad before they could get it away from us. At Keevil, though the theater was very much better and the mess had a well-stocked bar, the mess table swarmed with earwigs. In France, I was told, we would have dust and mosquitoes as well as all the forms of vermin known to man.

In Salisbury, Richard was able to join me for a few hours' leave. After all, he was then based only forty minutes away. We had so much to talk over, so many things to tell each other, as we strolled about the cathedral close. It was my last chance to see him before going to Normandy.

From the window of one of the ATS billets sounded a concertina, evidently being played by someone new to the art. "I'm dreaming of a white Christmas," wheezed the concertina. And four or five American G.I.s who were walking about, viewing the cathedral, grinned and started to whistle the song to help the concertina player. An elderly clergyman in a violet cassock, passing along a path to choir practice, looked first distressed at this invasion of the sanctity of the cloisters, then smiled benignly.

A lot of things were changing. Much of the England I had known and loved and had belonged to was gone. I had thought so many times, in the course of those five thousand miles which had taken me from Portsmouth to John o' Groats and back again. There was a house which once had been mine, a blackened mass of rubble with the wild grasses already claiming it for a ruin. There were the towns I had known and played in when they were thriving and intact, now maimed and disfigured. There were friends one asked about only to be told quietly, "Killed."

But all the changes were not sorrowful ones like these. Some, like the look on the priest's face when he smiled at the G.I.s, promised well for the future.

I said a little of this to Richard, and he agreed with me. Then we went on to talk of some of the many things which meant so much to both of us. Like so many husbands and wives in these wartimes, we had so little time. There was no knowing when or where—or even if—we would meet again.

After Richard left to return to duty and I packed up for the trip back to London to get ready for my trip to Normandy, my mind was full of the changes I could feel as well as see taking place on every side. I remembered how, as a child, I had thought of the world as very stable. Even boringly so. All the adventures, so I thought, had been had by others long ago. The grown-up people I observed seemed to live in a cut-and-dried world. They were already settled in life. In my heart of hearts I dreaded the time when this would happen to me. Yet people used to talk about "settling down" as though this were something every nice girl should wish to do.

Well, perhaps I'm not a nice girl. One reason why I have always loved the theater and why I'm still stage struck is that this sort of life offers variety, constant change, even dangerous and thrilling "ups" and "downs."

At heart I have always been an adventurer. The Danish strain in my blood makes me restless. I am a seeker, not a holder. I am filled with urgent curiosity about what may lie just around the corner.

During my illness in the hospital in Toronto and then throughout my prolonged convalescence, when it was bliss just to be alive with Philip in the sunshine, sometimes, even in the midst of my happiness, a chilling thought would strike me. Suppose *this* is the climax. The ultimate high moment. This is perfection. What more can life give me?

And even in the sunshine I would shiver slightly.

Philip was not given to introspection. He believed in taking life and people as he found them. And he found them good and fair to see. I never felt that he understood me particularly. Maybe I was too young to be very convincing. He had certain ideas about me which, put together, composed a personality, and he was in love with that. We never talked about our feelings. If I ever felt moved to tell him how I felt about life, the impulse withered immediately when I thought how Philip, with his social background, would receive such revelations. I knew it would have embarrassed him.

We were having lunch in the dark and dreary dining room of one of Cherbourg's small hotels while waiting for word that the *Aquitania* was coming into port. Our holiday was over. I was both sad and glad—sad because Philip and I had had such a happy time together. It could never be quite the same again. And I was glad, too, as Philip said, "Because you are going back to your job, Dormouse. I believe the theater means more to you than I do."

"Really?"

I said it, mimicking his accent, to make him smile. And he did. But inwardly I was wondering—as I did at times—if Philip was right about this. Perhaps he did know me better than I then knew myself.

16

THE POPULARITY of *Charlot's Revue* in America increased
the excitement and the warmth of our reception when we
reopened in London in the early spring of 1925. There was
so great a demand for seats for the première that Charlot
adopted the unique and daring plan of giving two performances—one at 8:00 P.M., the other at midnight.

Never was such an audience assembled in the theater as
at that second performance. Celebrities of society and stage
crowded the building from stall and dress circle to the
boxes, and even the gallery and pit.

It was the same show in general that we had played in
New York, and many of the numbers had been seen many
times in London, but it seemed as though everybody wanted
to see the familiar acts all over again.

Perhaps there was some curiosity as to whether playing
to American audiences for so long a run had changed Bea
Lillie's or my style. Bea was very much in the news because her husband, Bobby Peel, whom she had married in
1922, had just succeeded to the baronetcy. As Lady Peel,
Bea was an even greater hit than ever simply because she
remained the same unspoiled Bea Lillie.

The Guv'nor, as we used to call Charlot, was always
warning us that no artist can afford to rest on his laurels

until he is dead. He kept reminding us that he had not brought the company back to London merely to ride along indefinitely on the successes it had piled up in New York. He was determined to make the return of his revue the high spot of the season.

Bea and I injected into the *Revue* our joint impressions of the typical "sister act" which we had seen in America. This included a burlesque by Bea of Fanny Brice, and I did an imitation of Sophie Tucker, who was then enormously popular in London. For this act, Bea and I dressed alike, we played ukuleles, and of course we did close harmony. We were known as the Sisters Apple—Seedy and Cora.

One June night that season the after-theater crowds passing along Regent Street noticed a large car stop in front of "His Master's Voice" gramophone shop. The driver emerged from the car. After entering the shop, he returned with a porter in a green felt apron. The two men approached the car and the passers-by stopped and stared in horrified amazement to see the porter reach into the back seat of the car and, after a considerable struggle, bring out the body of a woman whose quaint crooked smile advertised her as Miss Beatrice Lillie of *Charlot's Revue!* As her gold-clad feet hung limp at one end and her arms were outstretched at the other, she did not seem in any condition to resist her captor. Her smile remained unperturbed and sweet as it faced the public over his brawny shoulder. He gently but hurriedly carried her into the shop. The crowd increased as word ran up and down the street that some queer happenings were going on. Once more the porter emerged. Again he dived into the car and came out with still another woman thrown carelessly across his shoulder. Someone said, "My God, it looks like Gertrude Lawrence!" The woman's legs kicked and her hands beat a helpless tattoo on his back, but the porter's powerful arms were folded tight across her rump. So finally he carried the two figures in and they stood side by side in all their gold-sequined glory as an advertisement for gramophone records.

"Blimey," someone in the crowd said. "They're dummies!"

"Not a bit of it. It's them."

The crowd argued and increased. Charlot had learned the power of advertising methods in the U.S.A.

Charlot's Revue ran for many months and then closed. Several months later Charlot had an offer to prepare another revue for New York, so he gathered his original company around him—Jack, Bea, and me.

Again we set sail for America—on the *Caronia*. Bea was accompanied by her husband, Bobby Peel, who was immediately surrounded by the press and was hard put to explain: first, that he was not a member of the company; second, that he was not connected with the London police force—the "Peelers," as they are nicknamed for Bobby's grandfather, who organized them; third, that he was no relation to "Do Ye Ken John Peel?"

When we opened in New York, Noel Coward was playing there in *The Vortex*. Our first night was very heartwarming—all the crowd turned up and Uncle Aleck Woollcott wrote in his column the next day, "It was not a performance—it was a reunion."

We had a good show. Bea sang "There's Life in the Old Girl Yet." Gertrude Ederle had just swum the Channel, and

Bea did a burlesque of that muscular lady which was hilarious. We did our "Fallen Babies" song dressed as one-year-olds, in huge baby carriages—ending up with getting tipsy from the gin in the feeding bottles belonging to our absent nursemaids. I sang "Carrie Was a Careful Girl" and "Parisienne Pierrot," both written by Noel. Jack, as always, was excellent, but for some reason the gilt was missing from the gingerbread. We ran only six months in New York and after a short tour we arrived in Hollywood. For three weeks the town was ours.

On the closing night we gradually noticed that all the Hollywood male stars in the orchestra seats were leaving before the finale. This worried us terribly; we couldn't understand such behavior! Well, Jack went on in his full Highland costume and sang the opening of the last song; I followed dressed as Flora MacDonald; and then came Bea as Bonnie Prince Charlie. By this time there wasn't a single Hollywood male star left out front. We all sang bravely and laughed gaily, trying to carry off our dismay, when suddenly one by one onto the stage came the missing males.

They all had their trousers rolled up to their knees; Valentino had on a Scotch headdress borrowed from the chorus girls; Charlie Chaplin had his dinner coat tied round his waist like a kilt; Richard Barthelmess had a tam o' shanter on; the Marx Brothers wore red beards; Jack Gilbert carried a ladder, for what reason no one knew. They took over the whole finale with us; they made speeches; and Chaplin, who at that time was refusing to make "talkies," made his speech in dumb show. Oh, what a night!

Bea stayed on in Hollywood for a while; she had signed on to appear in New York in September in a musical farce which Jerome Kern wrote for her. I, too, had made my decision to leave Charlot's management and accept a New York contract. That was to be *Oh, Kay!* produced by Alex Aarons and Vinton Freedley. George Gershwin was writing the music especially for me; and his brother, Ira, the lyrics. The book was by P. G. Wodehouse and Guy Bolton. Rehearsals were to begin in New York early in October, so I had time for only a brief holiday in England.

I caused some consternation when the press photographers caught me going aboard the *Mauretania* on a blistering August day with bare legs. I had experimented going stockingless in California and found it comfortable and economical.

As soon as it was reported that Gertrude Lawrence was going about barelegged, the papers began to interview fashion experts and other actresses to get their opinion of the fad I had started. Marilyn Miller, when interviewed, expressed ladylike disapproval of the innovation, and announced that she had brought back from Paris two hundred pairs of silk stockings which she had every intention of wearing. Miss Carmel Snow, fashion editor of *Harper's Bazaar*, was quoted as exclaiming with horror: "The idea is disgusting. It will never be done by nice people."

Pam came back with me when I returned to New York from England. My little daughter was a surprise to the American press, as I had never allowed her to be publicized or photographed for the illustrated papers. I wanted to keep Pam's life simple and sheltered, with no searchlights turned on her. I wanted her to grow up a normal, wholesome little girl and without contact with the theater. If she wanted to go on the stage later on, and showed an aptitude for it, that would be time enough to introduce her to the world in which I spent so much of my life.

Oh, Kay! opened in November and was a tremendous success. Gershwin's score was Gershwin at his sprightliest. The piece had lots of humor and that indefinable something which can only be described as spirit. Oscar Shaw played the lead, and Victor Moore provided most of the uproarious comedy.

It was that winter, my third in New York and during the run of *Oh, Kay!* that I met Bert Taylor, and immediately my life changed. This tall, dark-haired, stunning-looking American was like someone one only reads about. With a snap of his fingers, a glance, a quiet word, he had the power to bring about miracles. Bert had been born with a gold spoon in his mouth. His father was president of the New York Stock Exchange, and Bert had rolled up an enormous fortune of his own during those years when Wall Street was holding carnival.

Bert Taylor figuratively knocked me off my feet. From the moment of his entry into my life I began to live in a storybook world. While New York streets were glazed with ice and the sky sent down showers of sleet, my apartment was abloom with spring and the fragrance of American beauty roses.

A banker in Bert Taylor's position could, and not infrequently did, make a profit of fifty thousand dollars in a day's trading on the Stock Exchange; and, exhilarated by this achievement, on his way uptown to his club he would drop in at Cartier's and spend a part of the day's bag on a gorgeous bauble to please the lady of his heart.

Is it any wonder that Bert Taylor, who moved habitually

in this fantastically luxurious world, should have swept me off my feet? Philip and I were extraordinarily companionable. His devotion and attention to me had brought me great happiness. But from the start of our friendship both of us had known, and had admitted frankly, that we had no future together. Circumstances to which we both had to submit kept us apart. For several years I was content with half a loaf, but, as inevitably happens, the disappointment ultimately bred a restlessness. That, I really believe, was one reason why I wanted to stay on in America; and why I did stay on. It was no longer happiness enough just to be with Philip knowing that we could never marry and have a life together. I carried back with me to America a loneliness. Undoubtedly this made me even more susceptible than I would otherwise have been to Bert's great charm and to the attention he paid me.

I wrote Philip that I was seeing a lot of this young American. Philip and I had always been honest with each other. We were really and truly friends. Sooner or later he would have heard about Bert Taylor and me anyway. There were Americans constantly going over to London and to the Riviera and to St. Moritz for the winter sports, and many of Philip's friends came to New York. Bert's sister, the Countess de Frasso, was a well-known figure in the international set whose members floated from Santa Barbara to the Côte d'Azur, from New York to the Lido, and from Salzburg to Palm Beach.

When it was evident that *Oh, Kay!* was destined to stay on Broadway for many months, Philip cabled me that he was coming over to New York for a visit. And he did. In New York that winter for the first time he asked me to marry him. If he had only done so two years before I am sure I would have said "yes," and would have immediately gone about the business of getting a divorce from Frank.

Oh, I did not blame him. His career was as important as mine, and it would have been wrecked had he married a divorced woman. Though I was his wife, he could not have brought me to Court, since etiquette forbade this. He could not have entered the royal enclosure at Ascot—something which may seem petty to Americans but which is extremely important to English people of Philip's position, not merely for what it *is*, but for what it represents.

If I had been only an actress, we might have overcome some of the opposition, especially if I had abandoned my career and retired to Philip's house in the country. But I was not prepared to do this—not now. I belonged to the theater. My life, since I was ten, had been lived in it. The public had been kind to me and I owed them loyalty in return. Philip's income was not sufficient to pay the heavy expenses of his clubs, his uniforms, and all the obligations connected with his career in court circles and to support me and a growing daughter.

No, from whatever angle you considered it, marriage with Philip Astley was impossible.

So I said, "No, darling," when Philip asked me to marry him. Philip took the next boat back to England, and I went on with my job.

I sent for Mother. She arrived after "a beastly crossing, the worst in forty years. Even the captain was sick."

I had a beautiful apartment on Park Avenue with everything to give Mother a taste of American comfort and luxury. But she refused to approve of any of it. She complained that Pam had become too American.

From the beginning the idea was a mistake. Mother liked the apartment but it was too high up—it frightened her. She liked Bert, but she kept talking about Philip; she hated the cold weather, but she couldn't stand the steam heat. She liked her new clothes, but she couldn't understand Americans, and she never went out because the traffic all went the wrong way!

However, after a while she got more settled. Then she missed and worried about Dad. So when the good weather came, she went back to England. We hadn't discussed anything!

Once back home, people wrote me that she never stopped comparing the living conditions of London with New York; and the moment anything went wrong she would say, "Of course over in America everything is *so* different, and the central heating is *marvelous!*"

That summer I played *Oh, Kay!* in London and continued the fantastic existence I had entered upon in New York. Several Indian princes from Hyderabad with their entourages were at the Savoy and came to see our play. They adored it. The Gershwin score and the English company were excellent. The princes proceeded to show their enthusiasm by taking a box for the season. Occasionally the box would be occupied by several ladies in Indian dress, with their caste marks on their foreheads, precious stones on the sides of their nostrils, and beautiful long saris draped over their heads, swinging gracefully from their bejeweled shoulder pins.

The youngest prince took a fancy to me. We called him "Baby" because his own names were so many and so difficult to remember. Baby was enraptured by every sort of mechanical gadget and presented me with a cigarette lighter shaped like an airplane, and a miniature cannon which fired a lighted cigar. He bought dozens of such things to take home with him to adorn the palace at Hyderabad, where he invited me to visit him. He presented me with a very large photograph of himself on a very small polo pony.

Before going back to India the princes gave a banquet at the Savoy. It was all very sumptuous, and at every lady's place was a small gold kidskin bag.

I picked up mine. My fingers told me that inside were several small, round hard objects. "Ah!" I thought. "This is *it!* Nothing less than emeralds. Or pigeon-blood rubies." I shot Baby a questioning glance. He was beaming, confident of the great pleasure he was giving me.

"It is something you ladies like very much," he said. "I hope you like——"

I pulled the drawstring. Out into my expectant palm tumbled a handful of the betel nuts Indian women chew to blacken their teeth and gums.

I then and there decided not to visit Hyderabad.

George Gershwin was in London for the opening of *Oh, Kay!* and was lionized by English society. He gave concerts, he raised money for charities, he visited every famous "stately home of England," yet he remained the same serious, hard-working young man. He bought suits in Savile Row and took me along to the fittings and to select his shirts and ties at Hawes and Curtis's, and hats at Scott's. But he never lost his head size.

His one interest in life was his music. Before he returned to New York he visited France and wrote his famous "American in Paris" concerto.

I had leased a flat in Portland Place from the Marquis de Casa Maury and intended to make it my permanent home. Pam entered school at Roedean in Sussex. The flat was beautiful and I loved it. Sybil Colfax redecorated it for me. I had one of the first rooms in London to be done in mirrors, and a white drawing room with silver sequin curtains. I had gradually collected some fine old Bristol glass and some pictures, including a Gauguin. Also many photographs and bibelots. Among these was a charcoal drawing of an animal which was intended to be a pig, though it looked slightly like a rhino, and from another angle like a badger. It might have passed for one of Thurber's creations, but it was the work of the Prince of Wales, who drew it blindfolded, as a stunt at a charity bazaar, and presented it to me.

I didn't *buy* a Bentley car. I had one built. I took the Bentley to America with me when I returned late in the summer, on the same boat with George and Ira Gershwin, to start rehearsals for their new musical, *Treasure Girl*. I also took the very smallest baby Austin I could buy. I remember driving the Austin up Fifth Avenue one day and being stopped by a red light. The cop left his post in the center of traffic to come over and lean his elbows on the radiator.

"Say, lady," he remarked confidentially, "what do you do with it at night? Keep it under the bed?"

Clifton Webb and Walter Catlett played in *Treasure Girl* with me, but the show was not the success *Oh, Kay!* had been. I had one song which went over big, "Where's the Boy?"

All that winter and through the summer after *Treasure Girl* closed and I stayed on in New York to make a picture at Paramount's Long Island studios, I continued to see a great deal of Bert Taylor. Before coming to America, I had applied for my divorce, and the court had granted it, though under the British law the decree did not become absolute until six months had passed. Bert and I were engaged. He had come to London to see me while I was playing in *Oh, Kay!*, had proposed, and I had accepted him.

I was deeply happy; everything seemed to be coming my way. I was riding on the crest of the wave.

Gilbert Miller had signed me to co-star in *Candle-Light* with Leslie Howard and Reginald Owen. We were to open at the Empire Theatre in New York in the autumn of 1929. The play was a Viennese comedy by Siegfried Geyer, and had been adapted by P. G. Wodehouse, who had done so much toward the success of *Oh, Kay! Candle-Light* had been produced in London with Yvonne Arnaud in the leading role. It was one of the first of many plays—tragic and comic—written around the romantic figure of the Austrian Archduke Rudolf. Everyone predicted it would be a huge success on Broadway.

Candle-Light marked my first appearance in America in a legitimate play, and I was both excited and terrified. On the first night I had a cable from Noel, who was, as usual, going around the world on a tramp steamer.

LEGITIMATE AT LAST, DARLING. WON'T MOTHER BE PLEASED?

My pride knew no bounds when Gilbert Miller hung my portrait in the Empire Theatre with those of Doris Keane, Helen Hayes, and Ina Claire.

No one apparently, not even Bert, had any inkling that the autumn of 1929 was to be the end of an era.

I began to get the idea that money flowed in without restrictions or with very little effort on my part. When I remembered how hard I had worked to earn fifteen shillings a week just ten years back, it seemed incredible that I should be earning thirty-five hundred dollars a week in the theater. Not to mention my paper profits in the market. Of course I had no idea of it at the time, but I was to be one of the victims of the boom years. It was to be a long, hard time before I was to acquire a realistic attitude toward money.

Sometimes, when I had gambled successfully in the Street, I would remember poor Dad and his pathetic, ever-hopeful efforts to back a winner. He was still playing the horses. Mother shook her head over it, but whenever I was in England Dad and I would get together. He would confide to me his choice for the next Derby or the Manchester Handicap, and prove to me that his horse was sure to win. We were partners. He still considered Mother the most remarkable woman in the world. He would tell me so and would impress the same on Pamela:

"Your grandmother's a fine woman. And don't you go forgetting it, my girl!"

We opened in *Candle-Light* on the last night of September. Leslie Howard was excellent as Joseph. I shall never forget his way of replying to my question to the supposed archduke: "Do you, Prince Rudolf, have many mistresses?"

"Ah, Baroness, they do pile up."

In the supper scene Leslie and I were supposed to drink rather freely of the wine poured for us by the real archduke in the livery of a servant. According to theatrical custom this was really weak, cold tea and extremely nasty. It isn't easy to appear to enjoy drinking the kind of concoction the property man supplies for a rare vintage. One night I saw to it that the contents of the decanter were emptied and the bottle refilled with some excellent dry sherry.

After his first drink, Leslie threw me a look of delighted surprise. His acting took on added richness and flavor. And he tossed off his wine instead of toying with his glass as he usually did.

As for myself, I felt that I was giving the best performance I had ever given. I began to enjoy the supper scene. The archduke had to fill and refill our glasses. There was more realism than acting in the close of the scene in which Leslie and I became slightly spiffy.

Inevitably *Candle-Light* felt the impact of the crash that shattered the bubble of prosperity which Americans—and New Yorkers especially—had been playing with. But the play continued to run with more than fair success. Perhaps people wanted amusement that offered them an escape from their financial worries. They still did not want to face the grim reality.

Bert was up to his ears in worries and responsibilities. In the circumstances it seemed impractical for us to marry. At least Bert said it was. I was free to marry him and I wanted to, just to prove that I loved him and not his money.

But he said, "No, Peaches. I must fight this thing alone. I can't afford to marry now."

He had called me "Peaches" since soon after we met, which was at a time when the romance of a middle-aged gentleman named Daddy Browning and an outsize young girl called Peaches figured in the news. Bert was amused by the contrast my slim figure presented to the plump Peaches', and he enjoyed my fury whenever he called me the absurd name.

But now I did not retort, "Don't call me that." I protested I was willing to go on working to help things along financially. That only hurt his pride more deeply. We were at a deadlock.

When *Candle-Light* closed I went into Lew Leslie's *International Revue*, which had lyrics and music by Dorothy Fields and Jimmy McHugh. The cast included Harry Richman, Jack Pearl, and Anton Dolin, and, as the title implies, many continental and foreign performers. They all dropped out, however, after a few weeks, and only Jack, Pat Dolin, Harry, and I remained. You can imagine the sort of life those three madmen led me backstage.

I had two excellent numbers in the revue, "Exactly Like You," and "On the Sunny Side of the Street," that I sang with Harry Richman. But though a lot of money had been spent on the show it did only fair business. We closed in May. André Charlot had offered me a contract to star in a new revue he was staging. The offer tempted me; I was fond of the Guv'nor and owed him a great deal of my success.

It was always inspiring to work under the direction of this man of whom Sir James Barrie once said: "There goes the whole theatrical profession in a nutshell."

I signed the contract Charlot offered me. My plans for the next season seemed set. Then two men who had figured prominently in childhood years in the theater came back into my life.

17

THE TWO MEN were Charles B. Cochran and Noel Coward. They had a play which Noel had written. It was called *Private Lives*.

Noel had written it in Burma or Peiping or somewhere in the course of his travels in the Far East. But there was nothing oriental about *Private Lives*. It was modern, British, and suavely sophisticated.

When Noel's manager, Jack Wilson, brought me the script to read I fell in love with it. I was determined that I —and only I—should play Amanda, whose "heart was jagged with sophistication." Noel was to play the male lead, of course.

Noel wrote *Private Lives* especially for me. It was his fulfillment of a promise he had made to me and to himself when *Bitter Sweet* was produced and I was unable to play it because of my contract for *Candle-Light*. The part was given to Peggy Wood instead of to me, and Noel had said:

"Never mind, darling. I'll write another play, especially for us, that will be even better."

Now he had done it. But again I was under contract and did not know whether I could get out of my agreement with Charlot.

I dashed off a cable to Noel to tell him how thrilled I was

about the new play. I am usually reckless about cables and send terribly long, expensive ones. But for once I was having an economical streak, so I worded the message briefly:

> PLAY DELIGHTFUL STOP NOTHING WRONG THAT CAN'T BE FIXED

What I meant was that the only hindrance was my contract with André Charlot and that I was trying to get free of it, which I finally succeeded in doing. But Noel took it to mean that his pet play needed revisions. He was furious. The sputter of his wrath lighted up the Pacific as he journeyed, and he scorched the cable wires with scathing comments on my ability as critic and playwright.

We were right back at Miss Conti's squabbling over who should ride the bicycle and who should play the phonograph.

He was still indignant when he caught up with me at Captain Molyneux's villa at Cap d'Ail near Monte Carlo, which I and my friend Helen Downes had rented for the summer. Noel never has entirely forgiven me for that cable, and I don't think he has ever really believed even to this day that I was not making an adverse comment on his play.

We went over the play and rehearsed our scenes at the villa. Every evening we arranged and rearranged the furniture in the drawing room for a rehearsal. My other guests —among them G. B. Stern and William Powell—wandered in and out, amused themselves as they wished, and looked on Noel and me as on two quite pleasant but quite mad creatures.

Noel, Charles Cochran, and I decided to go into partnership on the play, so when we opened at the Phoenix Theatre it was:

C. C. L. *Present*
Noel Coward and Gertrude Lawrence
in
PRIVATE LIVES
An Intimate Comedy
by
NOEL COWARD

Noel had imbued me with the character of Amanda. In the cast with us were Everley Gregg, Laurence Olivier, and Adrianne Allen (then Mrs. Raymond Massey), and on the first night Noel gave me a specially bound and initialed set of all his plays, including *Private Lives*, which bore the dedication, "For Gertie, with my undying gratitude for her exquisite, polished, and sensitive performance of Amanda. Noel, 1930."

Everyone remembers the success of Noel's *Private Lives*, but we had our baby pains even with that for a brief moment. We have a very strict censorship guiding the destiny of all plays presented in England, and *Private Lives* had to pass the Lord Chamberlain's critical eye. So in due course the play was sent to Lord Cromer at St. James's Palace, and it came back with some criticism in regard to the scene on the sofa!

Of course without that scene *Private Lives* would have been like beef without mustard. We were all suddenly cast into the depths of despair. So Noel betook himself to Lord Cromer with permission to *read* the play.

Lord Cromer proved himself to be a man of great judgment in regard to what can be delivered to the public and in taking into consideration the manner in which the fare is served to them. So having enjoyed his afternoon with Noel and the delicate and charming treatment of the play, he gave us the green light, and not a word of Noel's script was censored.

So we opened in Edinburgh for the tryout, and Charles Cochran wrote me

. . . If there is another actress on the English stage who could give the performance you did on Monday night in Edinburgh, I don't know her. I am proud. I am happy—and I am grateful.

With affectionate regards, believe me, my Miracle Child,
Yours very sincerely,
CHARLES B. COCHRAN

Dear Charles Cochran. What a long time it was since I had been one of his children in *The Miracle!*

When we opened in London three weeks later, at the brand-new Phoenix Theatre in Charing Cross Road, *Private Lives* was already a huge success. The press made much of Noel. Lines from the play were quoted by smart people. When I, as Amanda, observed of myself: "I don't think I'm particularly complex, but I know I'm unreliable," hundreds of women snatched the line as referring to themselves.

I also stored up future trouble for myself. Ever since I played *Private Lives* people have been confusing me with the heroine of Noel's play. They think I must be brittle, irresponsible, and have the emotional stability of a shuttlecock.

Private Lives ran three months in London, even though it could have run much longer. Noel does not like long runs. We sailed on New Year's Eve to open at the Times Square Theatre in New York early in January 1931.

My clothes in the play were all made for me by Molyneux. He made me beautiful things, and Amanda did justice to them.

When we came to New York I brought along a sufficient number of dresses for use in the play to last six weeks. At the end of that period Molyneux sent me an entirely new set which I wore during the next six weeks. In this way my clothes were always fresh. And even though they were copied, we never changed their design. They were part and parcel of Amanda.

One of my properties was an extra-long cigarette holder, and this Edgar Wallace supplied. He kept me in holders, all marked E.W., for the run of the play.

I had expected Bert would meet me when we docked. But he did not. A radiogram to the ship told me he was at Palm Beach. In a few days he returned. When he did, I found him strangely different from the Bert who had seen me off to England the previous spring. He was distrait. He admitted he was terribly worried about the financial situation, which had grown worse instead of better. America was tobogganing into a depression, and no one, apparently, knew how to stop it. Like everyone else, I had lost my paper profits and a lot more. But I still had my work. *Private Lives* was repeating the success it had had in London.

One day I was lunching with Bert and some friends on Long Island. When we left the table I went into the powder room. I was seated in front of the mirror, putting on my lipstick, when I became aware of women's voices in the adjoining room.

"Did you see? That was Gertrude Lawrence."

"Really?"

"Yes, she's back. She's with Bert Taylor."

There was a little ripple of laughter.

"I wonder what the other one will do, now that Gertrude's back."

"It will be interesting to see . . ."

The voices floated off. A door slammed. Silence.

I sat and stared at my reflection, which stared back at me. Who was this "other one"? Was she the reason for the change I had found in Bert? I had to know.

I waited until I could stroll out nonchalantly and join Bert outside. We got into the car and headed for New York. I made conversation—gay, inconsequential. All the time I wondered how to introduce the subject which lay heavy on my heart.

We were nearly at our destination when Bert said something about the many changes which were taking place in America due to the financial depression. This gave me an opening. I asked him directly if his feeling for me had not changed. "I feel that it has, Bert."

He did not reply at once. His silence told me more than words could have told. So I went on desperately:

"Perhaps there is someone else now?"

"Well . . . I ought to have told you, darling. There is a girl I've been seeing a lot of . . ."

"I know," I said flatly.

He went on then to tell me about her. A pang shot

through me when he said: "I noticed her first because, in a way, she reminded me of you."

"Have you known her long?"

"No. Only quite recently. You were away, Peaches. You were gone so long. I missed you."

That brought another pang. And the memory of Philip. Philip had waited too long, and had lost me. Now I had stayed away too long and had lost Bert. I thought: people write plays about things like this. Poets write poems about it. And it's true. It really happens. If I had not stayed on in London to play *Private Lives,* if I had come back to America in the fall, Bert would not have found this girl whose first charm for him was that she made him think of me.

"You don't know how it is, Gertrude. When I come uptown in the afternoon, I'm tired. I want to relax, have dinner, play a little bridge or something, and then get to bed at a decent hour. I don't want to sit around alone all evening until your show is over to take you out to supper, and then sit up half the night. I have to be downtown early in the morning. I know it's too much to ask you to give up the theater for me," he ended.

Many women, I know, would have answered that wistful half question differently from the way I had to answer it. Between a young, handsome, charming millionaire and a career in the theater they would have found nothing to choose. In a sense, my own choice was made for me. It was made by that something in my blood which had made me spend two precious shillings to have cards printed:

LITTLE GERTIE LAWRENCE
Child Actress and Danseuse

which had pressed me to run away from home to seek my fortune with my father. That same compelling force had given me determination to stick it out with him through the distressing ups and downs.

Give up the theater? I couldn't. The theater was my world. I belonged to it. To ask me to abandon it was like asking a musician never to touch a piano or a violin again.

Everything that has value has its price. Nothing worth having is ever handed to you gratis. A career in the theater is no exception to this hard-and-fast rule.

The price of my career, I thought bitterly in the moment before I gave Bert his answer, has always been my personal happiness. Would this always be true? Would there never come a time when I could have a career and a happy marriage—as other women I knew?

"I offered to give it up once before, Bert, and you refused. Now I just can't. Not even for you. Also you aren't in love with me any more, are you?"

"I don't know," he said. "But I'm terribly fond of you, Peaches. I always shall be."

"I understand," I said. "It's for you to make the decision. You know now how I feel about you."

We left it like that. But it was the end, and I knew it. Sooner or later—and I suspected it would be sooner—the news that Bert Taylor and Gertrude Lawrence were "no longer that way about each other" would be a pointed paragraph for the gossip writers. If those two women I had overheard knew that Bert was interested in another girl, then others knew it. Or soon would. New York, like London, is in many respects a small town.

I told no one except Helen Downes, who often traveled

with me and, out of friendship, acted as my secretary. No one ever had a more loyal friend, and I knew I could count on her discretion. Noel was wonderfully understanding. He asked me lots of questions and gave me lots of good advice. One evening he said to me suddenly out of the blue, "I want to talk to you," and he followed me into my dressing room.

"You think your heart is broken. But it isn't. It's only your pride that is hurt."

I did not answer. My nerves were unsteady, and at this sign of friendship I felt the tears rise. I must not cry. Not over a man who had decided he did not want me. Yes, my pride *was* hurt. And I had woven dreams around Bert, dreams of a life together which Pam and his boy and girl could share. At least one part of me had wanted this from the earliest days. But there was another side to my nature which would not be denied—the side that was satisfied only by the theater and which could not give this up.

Philip had not understood this about me. Nor had Bert. Both had offered me security, and Bert great wealth with the security. But in each case at the price of my career.

I tried to get hold of myself, to steady my nerves. But I had lost weight and I could not sleep. I jumped when anyone spoke to me. One day I went to the doctor about my throat. He took one look at me and made his decision. I was put to bed in a private hospital. Noel was sent for and told I was too ill to go on that night. I would have to have at least a fortnight's rest.

Noel did a wonderful thing. He refused to play *Private Lives* with anyone else as Amanda. Instead, he took the unprecedented step of closing the show for two weeks. He and the others of the company ran down to Nassau for a holiday, and I meekly obeyed the doctor's orders.

When Noel came back he popped in to see me. I crowed at him:

"Look at me—I've gained ten pounds. I feel fit as a fiddle."

"You and your ten pounds," he snorted. "Look at me, my girl. Look at that tan." He pulled open his shirt to show me what the Nassau sun had done for his midriff. Then we came back to *Private Lives*. We agreed to reopen on the Monday after Easter.

Everyone said it simply could not be done. You couldn't reopen a popular play after a fortnight, and make it a success again. But we did. The last two months of the run of *Private Lives* were even more successful than the play had been at first. When Noel and I left the play early in June, my part was taken by Madge Kennedy and Noel's by Otto Kruger, and *Private Lives* continued its run on tour.

I was eager to go home. On the crossing I kept saying to myself: "I'm going home. Home. This time I shall stay." I had cabled my friends, including Philip, that I was coming, and their welcomes made me feel glad. Philip cabled he would meet me at Southampton. I looked forward to seeing him again. When I had played *Private Lives* in London I had seen him several times.

On the day before we were to get in I had a radiogram from him saying he could not meet me, as he had to go to the country, but would see me soon in London. I was disappointed, but could understand. Philip's father had died and he had more responsibilities now than formerly.

Mother was at the dock to meet me. She had brought Pam. We took the boat train up to London and I went to the Savoy. In those familiar surroundings I began to feel really at home.

The Savoy has always been a happy place for me. It was the first of London's big hotels I ever went into. I'll never forget, I ate my first oyster there. Lee White and Clay Smith had taken me there to lunch to celebrate my contract with André Charlot. They ordered oysters, which I had never eaten. I looked a bit fearfully at the things lying in their shells. I'd often heard it said: "You have to watch out for oysters."

Clay whispered to me: "They're alive. Or they're supposed to be."

I whispered back: "What happens if they aren't?"

"If you eat one you get ptomaine."

"Oh." I laid down my oyster fork. I was taking no risks about getting sick and losing that contract.

"Squirt a bit of lemon on them," Clay advised confidentially. "And watch. If the oyster squirms, that shows he's alive and you can eat him."

I squirted the lemon painstakingly on each of the creatures and scrutinized its reactions. Not a single oyster shuddered in its shell. All dead, I thought. Lor', suppose I'd eaten one. I watched Lee and Clay putting theirs away with no regard for the oysters' activity. All the rest of the day I expected one or both of my new friends to die of ptomaine. When nothing happened my cockney suspicions were roused and I asked someone else about oysters and their habits.

I put it down to pay Clay back for pulling my leg.

The six months I had spent in America seemed no more than six days. Each time the telephone rang, I thought it would be Philip, but it was not. On impulse I rang his house in Herefordshire, only to be told he was in London.

What did that mean?

He said he would be in the country and couldn't meet the boat.

I called his town house. Presently I heard his voice.

"Philip darling, is someone with you?"

"Yes."

"That means you can't talk freely now?"

"Yes. That's it."

"Very well. I understand. But I want you to know I'm at the Savoy."

"I'll come and take you out to dinner," he said. "It will be late. After eight-thirty."

"I'll wait," I promised.

When Philip arrived he brought me orchids. He gave them to me with the formal courtesy which was one of the things about him I always loved. He had a wonderful way at times of making even quite a small thing seem like an occasion. He kissed me and said how glad he was to see me. Then, as I opened the florist's box and took out the flowers, he stood by the mantel, looking not at me, but at the hearth, apparently engrossed in his own thoughts.

"Where would you like to dine?" he asked presently.

"What about downstairs?"

"No, no. The Ritz. It's quieter there."

We had dinner. He asked me about New York, and how the play had gone. I told him about Bert, and that we were no longer engaged. He said he was sorry and hoped I wasn't too unhappy about it. Then he asked about my plans for next season. We were like two people who had just been introduced. We were like strangers. There was something on his mind which he did not know how to tell me. I could see that.

When it got to be about eleven, Philip said abruptly: "I've got to be pushing off, Dormouse. I have to meet someone."

"Meeting someone?" I inquired. "Where?"

"Yes. At a theater."

"Oh."

Philip said slowly, "Madeleine Carroll. She's in a play at the Phoenix with Marie Tempest. I promised to stop for her and take her to a party."

"Oh."

It must have been my tone, for he said, as though he found it hard to get the words out: "I've asked her to marry me. We announced our engagement day before yesterday."

The day before yesterday! While I was still at sea. What a home-coming.

There was something more I had to know. I asked him how long he had been in love with Madeleine. He said, just a little while.

"Perhaps if you had come back sooner, Dormouse. You were away so long."

That was what Bert had said. And now Philip. Would I always be too late for happiness? I thought desperately.

18

IN THE course of the next few weeks I learned that though your chosen work may cost you heavily it comforts you in times of stress. Above all, if you are a woman and therefore apt to be emotional and personal, it compels you to be impersonal. It pulls you up by the bootstraps out of the bog of self-pity.

That is your reward.

And the reward is worth the price you pay for it. No matter how great. I found it so.

I held to my intention to remain in England for a number of years, and turned down several American offers. I felt I must re-identify myself with my own people and with the British theater.

I was working at top speed, and work was good. I played in *Take Two from One*, which had been translated from the Spanish of Martínez Sierra. The play was only fair, and the audience did not like me in a role which was so foreign to the parts I had played.

I had better luck with *Can the Leopard . . . ?* with Ian Hunter, at the Theatre Royal in the Haymarket that winter. I was the leopard of the title, an irresponsible, untidy, but fascinating lady whose husband tried, unsuccessfully, to reform her. The play, by Ronald Jeans, got good notices.

In that role I innovated a new fashion—an interesting

white lock swept away from the forehead. It caught on immediately. Women began flocking to the hairdresser's for a "Riviera bleach." If I couldn't change my spots, I could make the other girls wear my stripe.

I spent several weeks lazing in the hot sunshine at the Monte Carlo Beach Hotel reading John van Druten's new play. John called it *Behold We Live*, from the verse in St. Paul's epistle, "as dying, and, behold, we live." Gilbert Miller had arranged to produce it at the St. James's Theatre in August, with Sir Gerald du Maurier, Dame May Whitty, and me. Auriol Lee was to direct it.

The play unfolded the story of Sarah, a young lady with a past, who had attempted to commit suicide. Her case was turned over to an eminent K.C., who fell in love with her. His arguments made Sarah see that suicide is cowardly; that it is a bigger thing to live than to resort to firearms.

Marriage between Sarah and the K.C. was impossible, as he was already married. She became his mistress—a relationship which the man's mother understood and forgave. However, their happiness was blasted by the K.C.'s sudden illness. He was forced to undergo an operation, and died as a result. Sarah, unable to be with him at the last, was left alone to be comforted by, and to comfort, his mother.

It was a sad play, of course, but deeply moving and uplifting. Sir Gerald played the K.C. magnificently. The critics commented approvingly on my "restraint," which pleased me no end. Those same gentlemen of the press had written previously of my need to develop that quality.

At the première Lady du Maurier and two of her daughters, Daphne and Angela, were in the stage box, and came backstage to congratulate us all. But that was the only time

Lady du Maurier came to the play, which was strange, because she loved the theater. I often wondered about it. A few years later, when Sir Gerald died, I learned the reason. Sir Gerald suffered from the same incurable disease as the K.C. in our play. I do not think he knew this, but Lady du Maurier either knew it or suspected the truth. Naturally, she could not go to *Behold We Live* night after night to watch her husband portray his own destiny.

I felt that with *Behold We Live* I had reached a high spot in my career. I, who had begun in light musical comedy and revues, was now starring as a dramatic actress in a serious role with other truly great actors. I stopped in at Cartier's one day and ordered a pin for Auriol, to whom I was immensely grateful. I had it engraved with her name and "Behold We Live," and my initials. She wore it almost constantly until her death. In her will she bequeathed it back to me.

This Inconstancy, with Nigel Bruce and Leslie Banks, followed *Behold We Live*, at Wyndham's Theatre. When I went into my dressing room I experienced one of the high moments in my life. My name was on the door in gold letters, added to a long list of very famous stars who had been there in the past. Ellen Terry's name was there. And Marie Tempest's. And Irene Vanbrugh's.

While I was playing in *This Inconstancy* something happened which seemed unimportant at the time—just one of those things which happen every day, which are pleasant, but not momentous. One evening some friends came backstage to see me and brought with them a very tall, quiet young American whom they introduced as Richard Aldrich. Little did I know that he was to enter my life later on.

I was working terribly hard. I needed to. For one thing,

I was in debt. I had never recovered from the bad habit of spending lavishly. I know I am foolish about money. Some women are. I do not have a true sense of its value. Either I value it too much, so that I am actually stingy about a few funny things, or I spend a great deal too much.

I was pressed by creditors in England and in America. I was worried. I did all the work I could, including a film *No Funny Business*, which I made with Owen Nares. I went into business with two friends, Lady Diana Manners and Felicity Tree (Mrs. Cory Wright), and we opened a flower shop in Berkeley Square.

When I was a child the family used to discuss possible occupations for me. One of these was to be a young lady in a flower shop. This seemed to Mother a genteel vocation. And one which might lead to something. She reminded me that Cousin Ruby had risen from being a model at Harrod's to being a model for Raffel Kirchner. Cousin Ruby, through Kirchner's famous drawings, was the leading pin-up girl of World War I. Her pretty face smiled at Tommies from the walls of dugouts and trenches. From there to the Gaiety Theatre and marriage to Sir Henry Grayson's son had been but a few easy steps.

"Why can't *you* be like your cousin Ruby?"

Our flower shop was lovely with flower frescoes on the walls by Oliver Messel, the clever stage designer, and gay striped awnings. And it was popular. But it was also a lot of work, and I was busy with many things. I don't think it made me any money, though it was fun while it lasted. We called it "Fresh Flowers, Limited," and our friends called it "Faded Flowers, Incorporated."

Another way I took to increase my earnings was to write

some articles for the *Daily Mirror*. The paper said women readers would like to know my views on all sorts of things, so I gave them, freely. One day a feature writer discovered Pam at Roedean and asked her to give an interview on her mother. Pam was no more reluctant to do this than any normal schoolgirl would be. She gave the journalist a good story—about how her mother really disliked her work and would prefer to stay at home and live a quiet, retired life away from the stage, of which she was tired.

The paper printed it. It was rather awful. It took some living down and it took some explaining to make my daughter realize that publicity can be a two-edged sword and needs careful handling.

Meanwhile the bills and the dunning letters mounted. I had put some of my affairs into the hands of Fanny Holtzmann, the lawyer in New York to whom Noel Coward and Clifton Webb had recommended me. Fanny understood the theater and its people. She had helped me out of some difficulties when I was playing *Private Lives* in New York. But now she was in America. I thought, she'll be coming to London soon. She comes over often. I'll get hold of her then and get her to help me out of the muddle of my tax complications and bills.

That autumn Charles Cochran put on a play called *Nymph Errant* which was made from the novel of the same name by James Laver. It was the story of an English schoolgirl on her way home from school in Switzerland who met a Frenchman and set out with him on a series of adventures. These carried her ultimately into the most fantastic places. Incredibly, she came back at the end still wide-eyed, and quite unaware of what she had seen and escaped from. One of the amazing things about this story was that it was the work of a quiet, middle-aged scholar, who was head curator at the Victoria and Albert Museum.

I adored *Nymph Errant*. It has remained one of my favorite plays. Cole Porter wrote the music for it and Agnes de Mille arranged the ballets. I wanted to play it in America, and we would have done so but for the problem of financing such an elaborate production at a time when America was still in the throes of the depression.

Nymph Errant was a tremendous success in London. Nonetheless, I was worried. Not over the play or my future, but about my financial affairs; it seemed that the more money I made, the more I spent. I didn't seem able to get ahead, and my affairs were in a bewildering tangle.

Then the ax fell. The British Government came down on me for unpaid income taxes on my American earnings dating from some years back. As a British subject and resident I had not known that I was liable to taxation in both countries.

The news of my tax problems which appeared in the press opened the eyes of my creditors. All at once they descended on me. The straw that broke the camel's back was a laundry bill for fifty pounds. I could not pay it, and as a consequence I was forced into bankruptcy.

I understand that the British law which covers bankruptcies is much more severe than the law in America. I only know it was exceedingly stern with me. When I came out of Carey Street Court I had nothing, literally, but the clothes I stood in. Nothing else. My cars, my apartment, my jewels, even most of my clothes had been seized.

Fortunately the disaster did not affect Pam. Thanks to

that trust fund I had established for her long before. I never ceased to be glad of that.

There came a day when Dorothy, my faithful maid, Mack, my dog, and I stood on the pavement outside the house in Portland Place. We had literally not a roof to crawl under. No money and no credit. This was all the more extraordinary because I was appearing in a successful play—and on the surface was a successful actress.

Bill Linnett and Bill O'Bryen, who were my managers, came to our rescue. Bill Linnett offered me his flat in the Albany while he went to stay with Bill O'Bryen. It was a warm, friendly, encouraging gesture, and I shall never forget them for it.

It was up to me to start all over again, this time with a load of debts to pay off.

I did pay them off, all of them. It took me two years. I could have borrowed from friends, even from Noel, but something held me back. It was not just pride. It was a sincere desire to force myself to undergo the discipline which could be learned only by stern self-denial.

With the play still running, I started a film, which meant that at five-thirty every morning I was up and caught the workman's train to Denham to act in *Rembrandt* with Charles Laughton. After working all day at the studio I hurried back to the theater to go on in *Tonight at 8:30*. When the film was completed, I accepted an engagement at the Café de Paris, where I sang nightly after the theater.

Two years of work at that pace, and I was free of debt.

Noel brought *Tonight at 8:30* to New York. Immediately I landed in New York, I found myself faced by a new array of debts. It seems that under the British law I could be cleared of bankruptcy in that country while my debts in America remained unpaid. I had not known this. I thought I was done with it all, but I was not. I had to go through it all again—the unpleasant publicity, the prying into my affairs, the court proceedings. Again I turned to Fanny Holtzmann, but she was in Hollywood. Her brother David took over my affairs until she returned.

Between us we worked out an arrangement which left me free to do my own work, to finish the run of *Tonight at 8:30*, and then to go into Rachel Crothers' play *Susan and God*, while my financial and legal problems were taken over by the Holtzmann office.

Noel read the play and remarked: "The only good thing about it is the title." But I had been impressed by it when Rachel Crothers first read it to me. We talked it over. She agreed that several scenes had to be rewritten, and while she was doing this I ran home to England for the Coronation. I went with a peaceful mind. I was really free of debt at last, on both sides of the Atlantic. My affairs were in order.

I thought, that summer, holidaying in England: I'm a very lucky woman.

I have Pam. I have my work. I have friends, hopes for the future. I have lived a full, busy, active, and on the whole happy life.

I shall always be glad I saw London during the Coronation summer. It was wonderful—a last burst of splendor before the storm burst.

I came back to America to open in *Susan and God*, which played successfully on Broadway for two seasons. After its run, in 1939, I remember Samson Raphaelson trying to read me the script of his play *Skylark* while the radio in my living room gave forth the news of Munich. My heart was full of forebodings.

It was not long before those forebodings were justified. While I played in *Skylark* my country was plunged into war.

It made me restless and uneasy.

I was asked to play at the summer theater at Dennis on Cape Cod. The offer sounded delightful and I said I would go. I remember my trip by train. There was something exciting about it. I knew suddenly that I was embarking upon an adventure.

John Golden had recommended my going to play *Skylark* on the Cape. True to form and his love of showmanship he sent a fantastic story ahead of me, about the kind of woman I was. It gave the impression that I was an exotic creature who drank only champagne, demanded specially heated cars, and refused to sleep in any but her own extrafine sheets.

I have since been told that when Richard Aldrich, who was the producer for the Cape Playhouse, read this he exclaimed: "Oh, nuts."

I have never blamed him.

I got off the Cape Codder about half-past ten in the pitch dark. The man who led me to a car was noncommittal when I asked about my luggage and not very enthusiastic. This was the same Richard Aldrich whom I had met in London several years before. Though he was passably polite, I got the impression he was not overimpressed by me.

He told me he was driving me to the cottage which was to be mine for my stay. I could not see it, for there were no lights in the windows when we drove up. I began to feel that Cape Cod was a very standoffish place.

Mr. Aldrich guided me up the path and into the door. "Wait there and I'll switch on the lights."

I waited. The lights came on, and before my eyes grew used to them, people suddenly began popping out from under the tables, out of doors, from everywhere. Voices cried welcomes and "Surprise! Surprise!" It was a party to welcome me, and the leader of it was Jules Glaenzer, who had been my friend since my first winter in America. Among the guests were all the members of the Playhouse cast and Radie Harris, who was covering the opening for her radio program and her column in *Variety*.

I played at Dennis through that summer season. That winter, when I went about town, I had a new beau—Richard Aldrich. And a new happiness in my heart.

Richard and I took our time. We both wanted to be very, very sure. I had made one mistake in marriage. I did not want to make another. It was curious about Richard—it was as though he combined in one person the different things I had found and admired in Philip Astley and in Bert Taylor. He was Boston and Harvard, and had been a banker, but above all he loved the theater. He was the first man in my life who understood what my career in the theater meant to me—the first man who really understood me.

And so we were married. On the Fourth of July 1940. We chose this date because it had special significance for both of us. For Richard it was his country's birthday and for me it was my own.

For years I had said to myself: when I marry it is going to be a country wedding. I pictured myself being married in the evening in black lace and by candlelight.

We were married in the evening on the Cape. But in the pouring rain—Richard in white flannels and I in a gray sports suit. We ran through the sopping grass down to his cottage and were married there, with two friends and my maid Dorothy as witnesses.

Then, hand in hand, under one umbrella, we ran back up the path to the house of the Fran Harts, where friends were gathered to greet us.

So we were married. . . .

"And we will live happily ever after," I said to Richard. "If the war does not separate us."

"I know." My fingers tightened around his. The war was getting closer to America every week. At all times the thought of what was happening to London every night kept me grim company. "But if it comes, we'll take it together."

The next day I received a telegram from Noel Coward which said:

> *Dear Mrs. A.,*
> *Hooray, hooray,*
> *At last you are deflowered.*
> *On this as every other day*
> *I love you—Noel Coward*

To which I replied:

> *Dear Mr. C.,*
> *You know me.*
> *My parts I overact 'em.*
> *As for the flowers,*
> *I've searched for hours.*
> *Dorothy must have packed 'em.*

After we returned to New York I had to go into rehearsals for *Lady in the Dark*. Following this I went to Boston for the tryout. Richard was busy with his own productions. After *Lady in the Dark* had been successfully launched in New York, Richard and I moved into our new apartment* and looked forward to our life together.

Then came Pearl Harbor, and Richard, like millions of other husbands, volunteered to serve his country. He joined the Navy and went to war. I began to dream and plan how to get to the front too.

Note: On West Fifty-fourth Street, right opposite the house in which Bea and I shared our apartment in 1924.

19

SATURDAY, August 19, 1944. We are off at last. I am writing this by the roadside, where our convoy has halted by a clearing camp for the night. We are parked like all the invasion convoys we saw last June. We are over fifty trucks, jeeps, et cetera, and one hundred and ten artistes—the largest E.N.S.A. outfit to sail for Normandy.

We include Diana Wynyard, Jessie Matthews, Bobbie Andrews, Margaret Rutherford, Ivor Novello, and many others whose names I don't know yet, but who all seem in great form. Each unit or company has its own van, which includes beds and cook's galley. Part of my old unit is with me and we are conspicuous for the three fattest people in the convoy: Leslie, our pianist, two hundred and fifty pounds; Joe, the drummer, at almost that; and Zoë, who weighs in at just under two hundred and has comfortably given up worrying about it. These three, plus Zoë's husband, Basil, Clarence, the violinist, and I share one sleeping coach. The four men are in the tail end in bunks, then comes the lavatory; and the front portion and the galley are occupied by Zoë and me, with beds slung over the dining table like uppers in a Pullman. The officer and the corporal driver are sleeping in the camp by the side of the road. But it's pretty close quarters, and there are a lot of advantages in being

slender. Mary Barrett cried this morning when we left
E.N.S.A. headquarters at Hindhead. We all wished she
could have come with us, but from now on we are on our
own. We are now really and truly in the Army and subject
to rigid Army rules. Our escorting officer's name is Stokes,
so of course he is now known as "Pogis."

I have just been up the road and vamped some cup hooks
out of the local builder so we can hang things up in our
sleeper.

I have made up Zoë's bunk and my own, swept the floor,
and put everything I shall need under my pillow, as it will
be dark when we are called, and no lights must be shown
here or at the dock. I must remember not to sit bolt upright
suddenly in my bunk. The clearance is exactly two feet.

We were called at 3:30 A.M., rose, dressed in the dark, and
went to mess at the camp, carrying our own mess kits and
stumbling the half-mile down the road by torchlight.

Three E.N.S.A. units left for the port of embarkation
around 4:30 A.M. We returned to the convoy until nine-
thirty. When we got going, everybody was excited. We
rolled into Portsmouth at ten o'clock; our passports were
examined and we were issued "Geneva Cards," in which we
are rated as lieutenants in the British Army. This in case we
are taken prisoners. Before embarking on our LST, she was
loaded with tanks and our own equipment, and we had the
dubious pleasure of seeing several hundred German prisoners come ashore. Dubious, because they were a sorry, disillu-
sioned-looking lot. Among them was a small boy, nine years
old, in German uniform, said to be the son of a conscripted
Russian, who had refused to work for the enemy without

his boy. The mother had been killed. The British authorities were being kind to him, and he seemed very able to take care of himself, although he could not speak English or German, but kept saying "*Merci.*"

We are now actually "away" on our trip to France. It is a beautiful day, the crossing should be a good one, and it is good to get out of the coaches. We have had "muster," "Mae West" drill, and are now in the wardroom having tea while we clear the port—this for security reasons. The crossing is due to take about eighteen hours. So we sleep aboard, and are scheduled to arrive in Normandy "sometime Saturday."

A good night and a good breakfast at 7:00 A.M.

We have been joined by an enormous convoy and by mine sweepers, as we are now in the "mine path." The beaches are almost in sight.

I have been helping the Navy Red Cross to peel potatoes. They tell me that once on the other side these LSTs become hospital ships and are used to evacuate our own and German wounded prisoners. Most of the captured German officers are very arrogant and refuse medical treatment, injections, and even food, for fear of being poisoned. They have been taught to believe this. One wounded German aviator spat at our medical officers and kept asking, "How far England?" He was in great need of attention in general but refused to be treated. Finally one of the medical corpsmen said, "Now look 'ere, if you don't be'ave yerself, we'll send the lot of ye to London where the flying bombs are!" That did it! The sick bay is always down in the tank deck in a converted LST. They said you could hear that German's scream right up to the captain's bridge. Another member of the master race wanted to know how far the *Germans* had advanced into *Sussex!*

Our LST crossed like a bird, and we dropped anchor at twelve-thirty yesterday, nineteenth, at Courcelles, which was one of our first beachheads on D-Day. It all looked very quiet and far from warlike except for hundreds of ships of all sizes and shapes doing every kind of different job and the dreadful shambles made by the destruction of the German beach fortifications. We were a tank carrier, so we had to unload by opening the bow doors, letting down the ramp, et cetera. It's frightening at first to see the crew deliberately open the entire bow of the ship; one is sure the sea will rush in and sink the clumsy, heavily laden craft. We had to stand by until the tide was low enough for the tanks to take to the sands.

Some of the crew went over the side for a swim, and I wanted to. Perhaps I looked wistful, because the sailors aboard the U.S.LCT (6) 767, which was standing by, called across the water:

"Say, sister, why don't you go in?"

"I would," I called back, "if I had some trunks."

"We'll fix you up. Wait a sec."

Several pairs of hands were laid on a huge sailor. He was pushed, protestingly, behind a group which shielded him, and his yowls told that his capacious trunks had been pulled from him. The trunks, decidedly outsize, were tossed over to our deck.

The Yanks had dared me to come on in.

There was nothing for it but to find a secluded corner where I could slip out of my uniform and into the trunks.

They hung limply around me fore and aft. Zoë supplied a bra—one of her own and on the same scale as the trunks. I was safely pinned into it, a cap was produced from somewhere, and to the delighted shrieks of our E.N.S.A. members I was pushed forward to the rail.

With cheers from the Yanks I dived off the ramp and swam ashore to set foot on French soil for the first time since 1937. It was glorious.

I must stop here to tell the sequel to my swimming ashore on the Normandy beachhead. An account of it appeared in *Life* magazine. Shortly afterward the editors received a letter from Ensign J. W. Wray of the U.S.LCT (6) 767 of which the final paragraph read:

"The trunks which she borrowed from my 210-pound Mo.M.M. were most becomingly draped. We hope Miss Lawrence did not jettison the trunks during her tour of France, as we would like to have them back to suspend from the yardarm in memoriam."

The trunks were jettisoned, of course. Instead, I sent off to the crew of U.S.LCT (6) 767 a pair of my own pink silk lace-trimmed panties with the message:

Keep 'em flying until I can fill 'em.

As we beached we heard the news that the Allies had made another advance, which brought them to within three miles of Paris.

"Ssh!" said Bobbie Andrews. "I think I can hear Alice Delysia singing the 'Marseillaise' even from here."

Alice had gone across for E.N.S.A. a week ahead of us, and much had been made in the press about her picking up a handful of French soil and saying: "I shall not go back until I have thrown this over the Arc de Triomphe."

She has a fine record for her work with E.N.S.A. and, being French, she was naturally longing to get to Paris.

We drove in convoy from the beach to Masefield, which is a clearing depot. There we met Colonel Haggarth, our C.O., and were sent on to St. Aubin for four days. Ivor and the others have gone south to Bayeux. But we feel very superior because we're going "up the line."

On arriving at the village "estaminet," where our unit is in billet, two of my bags were missing. I motored back to Bayeux, hoping to retrieve them before the convoy split up. I went in a tiny jeep-sort of car known as a "Tilly" over twenty-two miles of invasion-made craters filled with oily mud. Captain Stokes Roberts drove, and we finally got there just as the convoy was pulling out for somewhere else. No halting is allowed on the roads, which are packed with stuff coming to and from the front line and the beaches. So we tacked onto the end of the convoy. After about three miles the line slowed down a bit and I jumped out of our Tilly and made a dash in search of the coach in which I had slept on the way from Hindhead. I scrambled aboard, flung open the cupboard, and there were my bags! I grabbed them, jumped off, and waited for my chance to dash back along the line. Then Captain Stokes Roberts reached out and yanked me and my baggage aboard. We pulled out of the convoy and returned—this time in pitch darkness—to St. Aubin.

That journey was terrific. Tracer bullets filled the sky. We met convoys coming from the beaches—all kinds of mysterious guns, cranes, stores, vanloads of German prisoners, and miles of Red Cross cars creeping along slowly in the dark so as not to jolt the wounded on the bad roads. We got back to the billet by midnight. No food, no light, and no water. But I had the bags, and a little brandy in a flask, and oh! boy, it was a lifesaver!

When I started to pin up my hair for the next day's show, I dropped a bobby pin. It sounds like a small thing, but in these circumstances they are as priceless as pearls. So I got out my flashlight, and there in its beam was my bobby pin and the sabot from a doll's foot—I shall keep it always for luck. I wonder what became of the child whose toy it was. But one learns not to ask questions.

We have been here at St. Aubin since we arrived in France, but we are doing two shows a day about eight kilos along the coast at Lion-sur-Mer. The place was occupied only a week ago and is a complete mess of mine craters, barbed wire, bombed and shelled houses, and each day the sea brings in its dead.

Our theater was once the Casino-sur-Mer, very gay and chocolate-boxy, but now it is all *Mer* and no Casino. The building is full of holes; no windows, no roof, no doors, and yet, somehow or other, we manage to put on a show. The men come in in hundreds. We are the first entertainers they've seen since D-Day.

This new life is going to be very strenuous. The food, when fresh, is often flyblown, and the canned food is always the same old Spam or bully beef à la something. Everyone has a touch of dysentery—very painful and most inconvenient. How I would love to lie down in a dark, quiet room somewhere with a hot-water bottle. I clean my own shoes, bring up my own water for my bath, and do my own laundry, when there is water. I never seem to quite catch up with myself or get any rest. But this is war as it really is, and I feel good and glad to be here.

The attitude of these Norman French is a little puzzling at times, but quite understandable in a way. At first these people (those who did not perish in the bombardment) were not at all sure that we could liberate them from the enemy. They felt that our landings would not be permanent, and that all this killing, loss of homes, and general chaos would be in vain; that the Germans would push us back again. Now that they know they are really free, they are more friendly to us. But even my Madame Martin said at *déjeuner* yesterday, "Mademoiselle, there were only forty Germans here in St. Aubin. All this destruction was not necessary." She was not a collaborationist—she has been evacuated from three different homes, but this was what she had been told, and she believed it.

Obviously, her informants were lying. I have been along the beaches and have seen the German defenses—the mines, the guns, and the famous West Wall. It took thousands of Germans to man all these. I have also seen our ships lying on the beaches with their sides blown out and their backs broken. And piles of knocked-out tanks whose occupants never even landed. The Norman Mesdames Martin are merely repeating, parrot-like, what the enemy told them.

It is very dangerous around here; several people were killed yesterday when a mine was washed up on the shore. Nobody drives or walks anywhere unless in another's tracks.

I hope to go to Caen on Sunday. In preparation I shall wash my hair at the officers' mess unit at Lion-sur-Mer today. They have electricity there, so I can get it dry.

Today is again Sunday and I have been in "Liberated France" exactly one week. If I thought I was in the Army before, I certainly know it now. We were to move farther up the line today, but the advance has been so rapid it is impossible to get to a place in time to catch up with the Army. So we are staying on in the Casino for one more week, and the men are to be brought back to us in trucks and lorries.

This morning we were put into an Army camp with the ATS and the NAAFI and R.A.S.C. I am writing this after curfew, by torchlight, in a room with plaster walls, bare boards, no bathroom of any sort, and my few belongings doing their best to give the place "the woman's touch"! I have put up some nails. It would seem the Army hangs everything up on the floor. We are "out of bounds for officers and troops," meals are eaten in mess, but we manage to have a lot of sort of school-dormitory fun.

There is another E.N.S.A. unit in this camp: Forsyth, Seaman, and Farrell. They are Americans but have been with E.N.S.A. for three or four years. They do a lot of outdoor shows and played only yesterday to seven thousand men!

It has been a most impressive day. The Doc and Captain John Bradshaw called for me at two-thirty in a jeep, and we set off to "do some shopping." We went to Cabourg— where only four days ago the Germans had been holding out. It was a dangerous and thrilling ride; we were all armed in case we ran into snipers. The roads are still mined on both sides, so no car could risk passing another, and along the way were many huge craters filled with the blood of human beings and cattle. There was no other car on the road going either way. I saw three French people on bicycles, pedaling back to see if they could find their homes or friends.

The little town was completely dead, no sign of life, not a shop standing, not a soul about, but everywhere the many German skull-and-crossbones signs saying *"Minen."* And fields full of the glider planes which had landed our airborne troops.

We drove on cautiously to the main street. Here the atmosphere was so eerie that I felt I had to speak in a whisper. The shops still stood there, although very much damaged. Captain Bradshaw had been in the town the day before and found two shops to which the people had returned, and he had brought chocolate and cigarettes for them. We parked the jeep, kept our hands on our guns, and stole quietly along the deserted street, keeping an eye open for any stray snipers.

At the door of a wine shop we stopped, and a dog barked from within. We spoke quietly in French and in English, and presently an iron grille in the door was opened by a young woman. She was alone, her husband a prisoner in Germany and her child and mother évacuées. We gave her chocolate and cigarettes and told her the news and we bought some wine from her.

We went next to the *pharmacie*. Here we found mother, father, daughter, and young son. All had stayed hidden during the siege. The shop was a complete wreck. However, in the cellar in an old brown leather bag we found perfume, powder, lipstick, and rouge, and we bought all they had. Each one of the family got something he wanted: the boy got chocolate; Papa got tobacco; Maman got cigarettes, and daughter got conversation. She spoke good English, having been to Farnborough near Aldershot for her holidays every summer in peacetime.

We gave them wine and then helped them bring back some of their furniture, which they had hidden in the cellar of a near-by house when the Germans first came. We left finally and promised to return when we could with white bread and marmalade. These people are still numb and cannot quite believe that they are free. On the way back we passed a few more stragglers returning, hoping to find something left. In one completely wrecked house I saw an old woman standing among all the rubble, with a *duster* in her hand! God only knows what she thought she could do, but her woman's instinct told her she should get started on something. She was, in a way, a symbol, and one I shall never forget.

Five years of war today. Our Army is eleven miles from the German frontier, across the Moselle, and the Gertrude Lawrence Unit has arrived in Deauville.

The ride here was torture—through Cabourg and its bomb craters (by misdirection), back again via Caen, trapped in a four-mile-long R.A.F. convoy—through miles of utter devastation. Bodies of dead Germans, looking like inflated rubber dolls, lie face down in the waters of the Orne.

Deauville is not badly damaged—it is just a dead seaside resort. The Hotel Normandie is prewar in its French atmosphere with good carpets, smart windows, and a wide brass bed and all its trimmings. However, it is all like a movie set—nothing works. Fancy fittings in the bathroom, but no water. Elaborate lamps and switches, but no elec-

tricity. Not even candles. A phantom hotel in a ghost town.
As there are no blackout curtains and we are forbidden
to use even a flashlight after dark, we decided to go to bed
while it was still light enough to unpack. I went to sleep.
Suddenly I was startled by a distant banging and sat bolt
upright in the dark. The knowledge that the enemy had
been here only four days before made me think "Gestapo"!
The banging continued, and I realized that it was no time
to disobey. I grabbed my flashlight from under the pillow
and stumbled to the door. Without opening it, I said, "*Qui
est là?*" A deep voice replied, "Open up. It's Hunt here."

I didn't know who Hunt was, but the voice was obviously British, so I opened the door a crack and said, "What
time is it, and what do you want?"

"I'm Lieutenant Hunt. You are to get dressed at once
and come with me!"

Definitely of the Gestapo species, I thought, but what
was the fuss about? Was I about to be court-martialed?

I turned on my flashlight, and there stood a very tired-
looking but determined R.A.S.C. officer who presented
me with our orders.

I realized instantly that this was an incident not to be
dismissed or handled alone, so in the murky darkness I
said, "Follow me, Lieutenant," and I took him along the
corridor to Basil and Zoë's room. Zoë was already in bed
and Basil was in the bathroom with a tiny bit of candle
trying to shave in a teacup of water which he had smuggled
from the dining room. We all pointed out to Lieutenant
Hunt that it was impossible for us to leave. Leslie and Joe
were still out somewhere.

It was then 10:45 P.M., and the order was for us to drive

by truck to the Seine, get across at 6:00 A.M., drive forty-five kilos to Amiens, and do a show on arrival.

The lieutenant looked us over, and Basil said, "Well, I don't know about anybody else's opinion. I have just washed my teeth and myself with half a cup of water. I'm going to finish shaving with the other half and then I'm going to bed."

Lieutenant Hunt saw our predicament, said he would return to Major Jamieson and make his report, and we all went back to bed to await court-martial! Next morning we hung about the hotel, not daring to leave and waiting for the summons to come.

We packed up and were ready for the worst. At 10:30 A.M. our new orders came and we started off with Captain Bayliss for St. Valery to join the column we'd missed the night before.

To reach St. Valery, we had to find a bridge or a ferry to take us across the Seine. We rattled along through the Breton Forest, past thousands of dead horses shot during the German retreat. We stopped at Quillebeuf, but the bridge had been blasted away and we were sent on. A Frenchwoman came running out, grasped my hand, and asked me to find her son in America and tell him she was safe and to please write to her. From there we moved on along the winding shore of the Seine which almost completes a circle at this point. No bridge remained intact and no ferry was running nearer than Rouen, a good ten hours away. We decided to go on to Grey's Ferry at Hauteville which our own R.E.s had built.

We paused at one-thirty in Pont-Audemer to eat and, as we were leaving, having given cigarettes to M. le patron and chocolate to the children, we saw a sign written on the wall of the café which read, "This establishment catered to the enemy during the war." We had been entertained and been fed by German collaborationists!

We shoved on again and finally reached Hauteville at about three o'clock. Here again was a sight I shall never forget—all the signs of utter chaos and frustrated flight which the enemy had left behind him. The stench was sickening.

We were told the ferry was not working, but "ducks" were crossing both ways with impertinent ease. It was decided that Captain Bayliss and I should thumb a ride over and find out what help we could get from the other side. So over we went, and found the ferry on the opposite bank in charge of Lieutenant Doug Allen and his company of Royal Canadian Engineers. He said the ferry was out of action but there was a pontoon raft which he was sending over for supplies. If we talked to Corporal Pete he would know if it would take our extra weight.

We found Corporal Pete having his dinner on the grass by the mess wagon. He was an enormous man.

He paused with his mouth full and stared at me.

"Don't I know you? I've seen you before, darned if I ain't."

"I've been in Canada," I said. "Several times."

Corporal Pete's face cleared. "Got it. It was at the Mount Royal. I can tell you the year. It was 1938. You was there lunching with Air Marshal Billy Bishop. You drank tomato juice. I remember that. And you did as well on it as lots of them do on scotch. You're Gertrude Lawrence. Shake." He held out a huge paw.

We shook, and—to show what tomato juice can accomplish—on the strength of it Corporal Pete agreed to ferry us across the Seine.

We sent word back across the river to the others that we were coming for them and hoped to get them and the vehicle across. The raft was floated by six pontoons and driven by four motors. She looked all right to us, until we saw the gang start to man the pumps! They pumped and pottered for two hours. "They always take in a little water after a while," said one of the R.E.s. Finally the raft was brought alongside, a duck was hitched to it by a towrope, and we were taken across. The party cheered as we arrived, and ramps were laid on the beach and we started to load up. Our coach got on first, then a jeep, then a supply lorry, then another jeep.

It was 7:00 P.M. as we cast off to cross the Seine. The current was running fast and strong away from where we wanted to go. However, it had been easy for the ducks, and the span wasn't very wide at this point. This time, to my silent dismay, we had no duck to aid us, and five minutes after casting off one of our four engines conked out. We started to drift with the heavy current. Three engines were going like mad, but we were making no headway whatever. A duck came alongside and threw us a line, but the tide was too strong and the towrope broke. We continued to lose ground, and finally Corporal Pete ordered the gang to throw out the anchor, saying we would ride where we were till help came.

By this time it was getting dark, a breeze was coming up, and I knew two things which I had not told the others. Each day the Seine is flooded by a bore which sweeps in from the Channel and causes a tidal wave twelve feet high. All light craft are cleared from the water at this time. The night before sixty-three persons had been drowned. The bore was due to come at midnight, and it was now nine o'clock and we were at anchor in midstream.

My heart was pounding and my senses alert to the danger.

Finally Corporal Pete decided to lift anchor and drift over to *any* part of the shore we could make and try to unload the raft before it got any later. I knew he meant before it got *too* late. He hoped to unload us all before the bore came down. We made the shore about a mile below where we should have landed, and wooden tracks were laid down. One jeep got off and away. Next came the lorry with supplies, but the bank was too steep and it got stuck. Just then, in the blackness, we heard the throb of motors, and dimly out of the darkness there loomed the shapes of two ducks. They came alongside, and it was decided to leave the lorry and get it by road the next morning. We put out into midstream again, the ducks were placed one in front towing and one at back pushing, and our own engines were running. It was now very, very cold and windy, but our spirits rose. We made a little headway, then the pontoons began to splash over. It was too dark to bale and we couldn't spare the men. It was now ten-thirty. All methods were used to get us moving, but the river was a raging torrent by this time, and the ducks were going round in circles, taking us with them.

Allen and Pete ordered, "Abandon ship and take to the ducks." The vehicles were lashed down, we grabbed our valuables, and all personnel took to the ducks and went hell for leather for the landing.

It's very strange, under stress, what one regards as valuable. I luckily was in battle dress (trousers, shirt, and short jacket), so I was sure of being able to swim. But my mind concentrated on the fact that, no matter if all was lost, my job was still to look glamorous, so I grabbed my make-up kit. After all, I can always do a show if I've got my false eyelashes. Clarence had saved his precious violin. Leslie had the music. But all else—including Joe Nicholls' five drums, our costumes and personal clothing—had to be abandoned. We finally reached the landing amid the cheers of the Canadian Engineer Corps who had been waiting for us, and we went ashore fifteen minutes before we heard the whine and rush of the bore.

We had to stay somewhere for the night and would have been content in the fields, but the bore had brought rain with it, so we were packed into trucks and taken to a deserted château which the enemy had taken over. Here were housed the refugees from the battle areas, and here we slept that night, huddled together on the bare boards, in our clothes; tired, dirty, but lucky to be alive. I wondered where Richard was.

Next morning we were awakened at seven by our Captain Bayliss to be told to "look outside." We did, and there in the courtyard stood our coach. The raft had ridden the bore and the Canadians had gone up at dawn with salvage ducks and brought the whole thing back to shore intact. We washed in the stables with the men, went to breakfast at the field kitchen, and then got under way on the road to St. Valery. We were all very tired, and I ached all over from the boards and the cold and the long hours on the crater roads, but now we were really arriving as ordered by H.Q.

We reached St. Valery only to find a completely dead and deserted town. Not a soldier or a civilian in sight. The water front was barricaded and marked "*Minen*," so we inquired of a sort of gendarme. He sent us to the mayor, who told us that the 51st Highland Division had left that morning for Le Havre to help with the siege. As we were supposed to be joining our E.N.S.A. column, which was entertaining the 52d Highland Division, we supposed we'd better follow on to Le Havre. Captain Bayliss said he didn't like the idea of taking us two women—Zoë and me— into that area without some confirmation from H.Q., so he and the corporal and two of our unit went off in our wagon to find the Army, while Zoë, Basil, Clarence, and I stayed behind at St. Valery. Clarence, who speaks French, went scrounging around and found an old couple who had just come back to their home. They boiled some water for us, and Zoë and I had our first decent wash since leaving Lion-sur-Mer almost à week ago! We left our bags with the old couple and went for a walk. Everywhere was to be seen destruction and the signs of the fierce street fighting before the enemy was driven out. We had no food with us, but we were again lucky and found the people at the Hôtel de la Gare willing to share a meal with us. We paid them, of course, and they were *très content* to have the British instead of the enemy. At three o'clock an aged gendarme rode into the square on a bicycle, dismounted, and rang a bell. Half a dozen bedraggled women, four children, and three old folks, and ourselves gathered round. With great ceremony he produced a dirty sheet of paper and began to read a proclamation that citizens should not go into the fields or touch anything because of mines; and that their claims for damage to property should be in at the mayor's office by Wednesday. He then rode slowly away, and the people drifted back out of sight again, back to the task of trying to make something out of nothing.

We hung about feeling very conspicuous and helpless. At five Captain Bayliss returned. They had been to Fécamp, but the 52d Highland Division was not there. From there they were sent to Etretat and finally caught up with it. But no sign of E.N.S.A. However, after he explained our plight, the C.O. agreed to send word down the line saying where we were and suggested that we join them at Etretat and give a show.

Without meaning to be, we are now the most advanced E.N.S.A. Unit. Basil, Zoë, and I are billeted over a plumber's shop. The others are at a hotel. Last night we gave two shows, one for the men just out of the line, and one for those going into battle at Le Havre, and then we were given supper at the mess and the pipers played and danced for us.

Today, September the seventh, we were to join our E.N.S.A. column and do an outdoor show, but a storm has come. It is dark and raining hard, so we are lying around awaiting orders. The visibility is bad and the men cannot fly.

These men of the 52d Highland Division are magnificent soldiers. They were at El Alamein, Sicily, Dunkirk, and have been in again since D-Day. They are having one swell time taking back the ground they were forced to lose in the early campaign. They swore they would come back again, and they have kept their word.

We shoved off again at 10:00 A.M. yesterday—got here

at Bolbec at twelve-thirty. The enemy held the town only six days ago. I went over to the theater to see what it was like, and as usual found no lights, no water, and everything soaking wet. We had three bulbs connected on a cord which had been given to us at Lion-sur-Mer by the R.E.M.E. So I got them out of the truck, connected them to one empty socket in the ceiling, and oh, wonder of wonders, they worked!

I then swept out the room, found an awful old carpet up on the stage and put it down amid clouds of dust and fleas. But at least Zoë and I had some sort of a room to dress in. We have no manager or stage manager with us. Leslie has to tune the piano always and often has to go out and *find* one. We all do everything for ourselves, and I'm the one who does the scrounging.

I found an old Frenchwoman on the way to the theater who was ironing in her window. So I went in, offered her some soap flakes which I had, and she promised to do some laundry for us. It is getting colder.

We are giving two shows a day, at three o'clock and at six-thirty, and the place is *jammed*. They come in direct from the line, some all bound up, dirty, tired, but all in great spirits, and they sing as though their lungs must burst. It's great to be with them, and all grouses disappear once the show is on. If they can take it, we most surely can. I have only a little more time over here before returning to London and to the U.S.A. to fulfill my contract. But hardships all considered, I am beginning to wish I could stay, and hang my panties on the Siegfried Line.

I wish somebody—anybody—could come and see what our little unit can do. Three in the orchestra—piano, violin,

and drums. And three others—Basil, Zoë, and me. No bally-
hoo, no fuss, no publicity. In the daytime we share our
rations of white bread, chocolate, and cigarettes with the
village children. They have had no white bread since the
German occupation—some have never before tasted chocolate. The eternal cry is "Cigarettes for Papa." The évacués
still are coming in on foot from Le Havre. I got my new
ration of chocolate, sweets, and biscuits today, and took
them down to the street outside our hotel. The children
appeared from everywhere like London sparrows, and the
ration is now *fini!*

Last night we had supper at the château now occupied
by the Royal Artillery Anti-Tank Corps. It was exciting
because several of the officers had just come back from Le
Havre where they saw the surrender of the German general.

There was a wood fire blazing in the great fireplace of the
château and I practically sat in it. The cold, penetrating
dampness is becoming worse each day. I have no warm
pajamas or cardigan and can't get any. Today I lined my
shoes with newspaper to keep my feet warm. I dare not
risk catching a cold or even the sniffles. My job is to sing
and look glamorous. Not too easy in the conditions we are
living and traveling under.

When I heard they had a real bath with hot water at
the château I immediately set about making myself as
charming and popular as possible to soften up the territory
preparatory to making a request for a half-hour in the tub.

Later: Alas, for my hopes of a bath. The heavy tanks
coming from Le Havre have broken the water mains.

This business of being without water is worse than all
other discomforts. We all have *l'estomac de Normandie*

again, and the sanitary facilities are practically nonexistent.

I discovered a row of three evil-smelling, ramshackle outhouses, all open at the top, behind the theater where we are doing our show. These were used by troops and civilians. The arrangement is decidedly primitive—no seat, just a hole in the ground and two places for your feet. You simply crouch and let nature take its course.

Humiliating as it was to have to resort to these measures, I could have borne that had I not suddenly become aware that I was not alone. The cubicle beside mine was also occupied. There I stood, undecided whether to make a dash for it or to wait until the man left. If I dashed, I might run into him. I could only pray that when I made my entrance on the line: "Here she comes, our own glamorous Gertrude Lawrence," my neighbor would not recognize me from our last informal meeting!

So I stayed. Hours, it seemed. Men came and went. Dysentery is no respecter of persons. Finally, with only fifteen minutes to show time, I bolted from my cubicle, like the mechanical hare at a greyhound race, and sprinted over the uneven ground to the back door of the theater. I was safe.

Yesterday at Foreshon the stage was twelve feet from the floor. No one had fixed the lights and everything was filthy. Zoë and I wanted to get our things into the dressing room but could do nothing in the dark. While waiting for an electrician to turn up, we pulled off our coats and pushed the seats closer to the stage. We were only six entertainers in that vast place. Even if the "mike" could be made to work, we had to have the men nearer to us.

Still no one showed up to fix the lights.

"Let's see what we can do," said Zoë.

Armed with flashlights, she and I went below and poked about in the debris until we discovered a small room with a sink and one electric-light socket. We attached to this our three bulbs on their flexible cord. Those emergency lights and my make-up kit were the most important part of my baggage. We tied the cord to a pipe running round the room and hoped the bulbs would work if—and when—the juice was turned on.

By this time the men were already lining up for the show. The first comers lifted the piano onto the stage for us. Meanwhile, Basil arrived and put up two posters so the men would know what they were going to see.

At this moment the electrician showed up. He informed us that the lighting system was controlled from Bolbec, six miles away. He had to go there to get permission to turn it on, *if it would turn on.*

He left, and we sat down to wait, dirty, tired, and frayed at the nerve ends. No one was in a welcoming mood when the Public Relations officer put in an appearance and said, reproachfully, he had the cameraman in tow and they had been chasing us all over France. And would we please come out at once and have the pictures done. You don't say "I won't" to a three-pipper, so we posed with the boys. I tried to look glamorous, though most of my make-up was gone, and the dust of the cellar had not improved my appearance.

Finally the lights came on, and we all rushed below to dress. The men poured into the theater, and once again the spirit of the trouper rose to its usual heights.

Just as we were about to begin, our driver discovered that the "mike" was not working again. It was too late to do anything about it, the show had to go on. So we started, but one by one we died at our posts. Not a sound could be heard from any of us in that huge place. The men became restless, and no wonder.

We got it over, and then I struck. "No show tonight unless the mike is fixed." After all, as someone pointed out, there were some six hundred technicians within call, who could easily fix the mike for us.

We were drinking welcome cups of real tea—our first since leaving England—when suddenly a voice boomed out above us: "Hello, testing. Hello, testing."

A sergeant had changed a valve in the mike outfit and it worked.

So we put on another show at once for the newly arrived audience.

This time everything started beautifully. The overture was O.K. We heard Clarence announce: "Joe Nicholls, the well-known London drummer." At this every light in the place went off.

Zoë and I sat in our dressing room in stunned silence, knowing that the switch was controlled from Bolbec, six miles away.

We could hear Joe drumming in the dark. How did he do it? We found out later—he stood close to the mike and played on his big strong teeth! And he kept it up until the lights came on again. We finished the show.

The E.N.S.A. shows are supposed to be only for the troops. Now and then you see a civilian seated among the boys. There was one little old lady in the audience at Etretat. She had billeted our unit and had helped us greatly. During the four years of German occupation she had refused to see a show. Now she sat in the front row, smiling broadly and trying to join in the singing of "Tipperary," while the tears rolled down her cheeks.

Driving north toward Belgium, we made a triumphal progress through towns which had been in German hands only a few days before.

As we made our way slowly down the main street, avoiding a few shell holes, men, women, and children turned out to greet us. We all bowed and smiled.

"I know now how the Queen feels at the opening of Parliament," said Zoë.

Our destination was Brussels. Other than that we knew nothing. But it was enough. Brussels had just been liberated, the front was very close, we would be entertaining men straight from the fighting line. At Lille, where we put up for the night, no billets had been arranged for us, as the enemy had withdrawn too short a time before. However, Clarence knew the city and was able to guide us to a hotel where they made room for us. Everywhere people were breathless at the speed with which the Allies were advancing.

Just before the outskirts of Brussels Bayliss said: "There's Major Jamieson." He had just passed us in his jeep and honked for us to stop. Our spirits were in good shape but our stomachs were empty. This seemed a happy chance, and Captain Bayliss got out. While he and Jamieson met in private conference, we sat like good children in a school bus and waited.

Then Jamieson came to the door of our car and said, "Everything all right?" I suppose we nodded, and he went on gaily: "Wonderful hotel for you all laid on in Brussels. Glorious new theater. There's hot and cold water. And light. Mrs. Herbert is there."

We stared at him. It sounded too good to be true—*hot and cold water!*

He then dashed off and we crashed into a flood of questions to Bayliss: "Where are we staying? For how long?"

"I don't know. My orders are to deliver you to Colonel Haggarth on arrival, and the show is at seven-thirty tonight."

We had by now come two hundred and sixty miles, had started off that morning without even a warm drink. It was already one-fifteen and we had to report to the colonel even before going to our hotel. On top of this, we were expected to give a performance at night in clothes that had been packed up for two days. Everybody in the coach vowed that there could not possibly be a show that night.

Brussels was holding carnival with flags, crowds, and the White Brigade patrolling the streets, rounding up collaborationists.

As our truck came to a standstill in the Grand' Place, people gathered around, demanding to know the meaning of E.N.S.A. on our shoulders. None of us could tell them, so we got out, did a few dance steps, and said "Cabaret."

They understood that all right. To make it all clear I added:

"*Cabaret pour le soldat.*"

A cheer went up. Then immediately a clamor began: "*Cigarettes? Chocolat? Savon?*" Hundreds of hands stretched out.

Savon—soap—was what I wanted too. That and gallons

of hot water, and a bed to stretch my aching body on. Captain Bayliss had gone in search of the colonel to report us and there were no signs of his return. Basil was in a towering rage, Zoë fidgeted—she wanted to go to the lavatory and nobody could find one. Clarence and Joe and Leslie philosophically went to sleep.

Presently Bayliss came back and said the colonel was at lunch, but a corporal had told him we were all billeted at the Hotel Metropole, which turned out to be a vast place but completely deserted. The proprietor looked uneasy and said a room had been booked for Miss Lawrence, but none for the rest of the party. This was strange and a bit terrifying when I found out—as I soon did—that the hotel was being boycotted by the Belgians as the proprietors were said to be collaborationists.

I did not at all like the idea of staying there by myself.

However, I was famished, and the Metropole had food—soup, salmon with mayonnaise, and dessert. Price per person, one hundred francs. We were just beginning on this ruinously expensive meal when in walked Lieutenant Charles Rogers, whom we'd last seen in the Orkneys. He said the others had been billeted at the Royal Nord, and I said quickly:

"Then I'll go there. They'll have to find a place for me there. I won't stay anywhere without my unit."

He agreed to take me, and then we got out all our money to pay our lunch bill. There was a fuss over this, as neither Bayliss nor I nor Charles Rogers had any Belgian money, and the proprietor at first refused to accept French money.

We were impatient to get going and to unpack because Charles had told us we had to give a show that night. Fourteen thousand troops were in the city. Prince Bernhard of the Netherlands was also there to celebrate the landing of British air-borne troops in Holland.

"I came here to entertain the troops, not to entertain royalty," I said snappily. "But if it's an Army order——"

"It is," said Charles.

Finally we got away from the horrible Metropole and I was given a room at the Royal Nord with the gang.

Brussels had a curfew. We were warned that a lot of shootings took place at night. Our soldiers went about with rifles. The city had no tea, no coffee, no butter, no bread. But it had water and lights. And real, clean beds. Breakfast next morning was doubtful. I made a glass of tea in my room and drank it with a German field-ration biscuit which we had found at Lion-sur-Mer and which I had brought along as a souvenir. The tea—one teaspoonful of the real commodity—was given me by Zoë. I made a tea bag of make-up muslin and heated the water in my field mess can on a German stove.

The performance that night was in a theater about the size of the Radio City Music Hall in New York. So long as the Germans occupied Brussels, Belgians were not allowed there, so, since we took over, the colonel had decided civilians should be admitted to shows. A van with a loudspeaker announcing the show had gone through the streets, so the house was filled. *But* no troops. And no Prince Bernhard. Just a few R.A.F. on the side aisles.

Of course we did the show in English. It didn't matter when we sang. But Basil, who is a patter comedian, was up against it. He solved this by raising his opera hat when he came on and saying politely, *"Vive la Belgique."*

That brought enormous applause, and after that whatever Basil said was received enthusiastically by the audience who could not have understood a single word of it.

At seven-thirty last night—in the theater, while I was waiting to go on—none other than Colonel Haggarth *himself* came to me with an urgent plea that I stay for another three days and go into Antwerp! Three thousand Canadians have just come in from the front line, and even though the enemy was only three miles outside the city they wanted a show and had asked for the Gertrude Lawrence Unit.

I quickly wrote out two cables to be sent through the War Office in London: one to Gilbert Miller, who was expecting me daily to start rehearsals on a new play, and the other to Richard, telling of the colonel's request.

We drove the forty-five kilometers from Brussels to Antwerp and put on our shows at the E.N.S.A. Music Hall. It was my farewell performance on the Western Front, and it was played to the accompaniment of gunfire. British tanks of the Guards' armored division had captured the city proper just twenty days before, but the Germans were still in command of the suburb of Merxem. This put Von Rundstedt approximately three thousand yards from the theater.

The hall was packed with Canadians and a dash of British and Yanks. I made my entrance to the last eight bars of "Some Day I'll Find You," and swung immediately into "A Lovely Way to Spend an Evening."

"Isn't it," I thought, as a shell burst close by. I asked over the footlights: "Is there a Joe in the house? Anybody here named Joe?"

Of course there was; there always is. He was sitting in the

second row, which made it easy to sing directly to him: "A Guy Named Joe." He slumped down in his seat and I could see his neck and ears get red, but the other fellows enjoyed his discomfiture as much as the song itself and joined in the chorus. Then an E.N.S.A. corporal unrolled a placard with the words of the song on it.

I called on six soldiers from the front row to help hold the placard. They leaped the footlights, among them Joe from the second row. We put on an impromptu skirmish, to the delight of the rest of the house, and the six went back to their seats with an imprint of my best lipstick on their cheeks.

I used up a lot of lipstick on my tour of the Western Front. In camps where we played two shows in quick succession I decorated more soldiers than General Eisenhower had to date.

The program ended with a singsong, including "Irish Eyes," "You Made Me Love You," "Wee Doch-an-Dorris," and "Tipperary." Finally we sang "I'll See You Again," and I thought to myself: it's a promise and a prayer.

I am writing this in the plane on my way back to America.

My service on the Western Front is over. I hope I have repaid some of what I owed to those British Tommies of World War I who dug into their breeches pockets and brought forth the half crowns and shillings that paid my fare to London and my first real chance in *Charlot's Revue*.

England is my country, but I am married to an American. Now that I have done my bit for E.N.S.A., I hope the

U.S.O. will send me out with a show to entertain the American boys. I would like to serve both countries that I love and belong to.

The Atlantic, which seems not nearly so wide now as it once was, is below me at this minute. Our plane purrs softly through banks of cloud. Its shining nose is pointed westward.

The skipper has just paused beside my seat and whispered confidentially: "Lunch in New York tomorrow."